DOG DAYS

Aidan Higgins was born in 1927. *Langrishe, Go Down*, his first novel, won the James Tait Black Memorial Prize and the Irish Academy of Letters Award, and was later filmed for television with a screenplay by Harold Pinter. His second novel, *Balcony of Europe*, was shortlisted for the 1972 Booker Prize. The novel *Lions of the Grunewald* appeared in 1993 and a collection of shorter fiction, *Flotsam and Jetsam*, in 1996. *Donkey's Years* (1995) was the first volume in a planned trilogy of the Higgins Bestiary of which *Dog Days* is the second, concluding with *The Whole Hog*.

ALSO BY AIDAN HIGGINS

AIDAN HIGGINS

Dog Days

A Sequel to

Donkey's Years

For Jane
Affectionately

Rory

VINTAGE

Published by Vintage 1999

2 4 6 8 10 9 7 5 3 1

First published in Great Britain in 1998
by Secker & Warburg

Vintage
Random House, 20 Vauxhall Bridge Road, London SW1V 2SA

Random House Australia (Pty) Limited
20 Alfred Street, Milsons Point, Sydney,
New South Wales 2061, Australia

Random House New Zealand Limited
18 Poland Road, Glenfield,
Auckland 10, New Zealand

Random House South Africa (Pty) Limited
Endulini, 5A Jubilee Road, Parktown 2193, South Africa

Random House UK Limited Reg. No. 954009

A CIP catalogue record for this book
is available from the British Library

ISBN 0 09 927492 2

Papers used by Random House UK Limited are natural,
recyclable products made from wood grown in
sustainable forests. The manufacturing processes
conform to the environmental regulations of the
country of origin.

Typeset in Bembo by MATS, Southend-on-Sea, Essex
Printed and bound in Great Britain by
Cox & Wyman Ltd, Reading, Berkshire

For Zin,
on the sunny side of
the street.

Contents

PART I: First Love

PART II: No. 11 Springhill Park

PART III: Ballymona Lodge, 1985

. . . in the hoax that joke bilked.
James Joyce,

Finnegans Wake

PART I:

First Love

The Happy Hours

First love, then the pharmacy.
E. M. Cioran

In those neverending summery days of endless dalliance in the dunes, neverending but brought to a decent close only with the coming of dusk, in the cool of the evening with the sun going down at last, when hand in hand we wended our slow way home along the railway track that ran parallel to the shore, until we came to where the little stream flowed out into the sea, all was tranquil.

Our unchained bikes were propped up against the broken fence, one lying on top of the other as if engaged in rapt and silent copulation, the heavy Raleigh model on top, the dainty female model underneath. From there we cycled alongside the south beach, to make our not so different ways home.

Drained and sated by her and the sea I cycled back to the brokendown bungalow on Kinlen Road on the edge of the Burnaby, still tasting and inhaling her homemade lobster mayo on my positively tingling fingertips.

Meanwhile Philippa with inflamed cheeks fairly cauterised by persistent kissing, made salty and sticky with seaspray and tangy fish scales, was being slyly admired by the lecherous Scuffle from his little cabin or observation post by the railway station. Portly and wheezing he saw and admired the twin dimples of her bum ('my boh'hum') as she flew by, offering him an alluring last glimpse of her fareyouwell behind fairly moulded into ice-blue poplin slacks which she had run up herself, the clever thing, on her mother's sewing machine; tight-fitting slacks out of which her buttocks were fairly bursting, as she flew by, showing off deep dimples.

Philippa wore nothing much at her ironing. She was more a small brown wren than she was a wagtail, darting from her bush, twittering, flitting from point to point, racked with nerves, troubled by foddering.

When she applied lipstick she puckered up her Clara Bow lips to get it even, a little red purse for her small change. Once she had a boil on her bottom that had to be lanced by Dr Wylie, for whom she must have obligingly raised her shorty nightdress and lain on her stomach to be lanced.

My brown hedge-warbler stood at the ironing-board in her bra and panties and sang a little song under her breath, running the grace notes all together with trills and runs, rumpily ta-thumping and ironing carefully dampened skimpies while throwing me a fiery look of disfavour; wasn't I the really low one!

Her plump rump, let it be said, was twice the size of her bust and deeply indented with dimples provocative as nipples, beslubbered with kisses.

She had been a late baby; later again a Montessori in-structress; hers a complacently lazy mind. I read Herrick to her, lent her *Fanny Hill*.

But she was beyond corruption. *Coitus interruptus* became our *modus vivendi*; it had in it elements of the carnal, as we came to our pleasures by ways circuitous, that were our own ways.

'Naughty!' groaned stoutly perspiring Scuffle, clasping himself manfully under the service counter on which were scattered the dismantled parts of a bicycle and repair kit, French chalk and inner tubing.

To every crochet its quaver; for look you now she has dismounted to purchase something, some essentially female thing, from Johnston the chemist. Tampons, underarm roll-on, mouth detergent, creams, pills.

But a late date on the harbour wall? Not on your life. I

must be out of my mind. What did I take her for, indeed! One of the slack-mouthed local trulls, common little tarts, or what? Who did I think she was? Whom did I take her for? She, the refined lady sixteen summers my senior, thirty-eight to my rising upstart twenty-three and not long out of college, at that. We met in the little seaside resort.

Philippa might just have resembled Murphy's Celia in being ('for an Irish girl') 'quite exceptionally anthropoid', when it suited her. She was a Montessori mistress and mine too, in a way, all nine stone six ounces of fragrant womanhood, come what may. Every licence allowed by lissom lady, from oyster-kissing to manual masturbation, but full frontal assault and penetration was rather frowned upon and the cunt proper definitely *verboten*. These were her strange ways; just so much and no more, be satisfied with what you got. Her religion (was she not a practising Catholic who went to confession and took communion?) forbade it. She would not brook it, could not go the whole hog.

'Be good.'

Where does that take us? Where does one go from there, messmates? Who declared that it was possible to wear away the night with all importunity, just by kissing and plain touching, without consummation? Isn't it in Old Burton's *Anatomy of Melancholy*?

We were stuck together naked as limpets for hours at a stretch, clenched tight as clams in the windy dunes, lost in the bracken, in the ferns, in the long grass by the faraway beach; until I had almost worn away her patience, her resistance; until Mother Nature herself, grown even more benevolent, had succumbed, become emblem all incandescent and azure above and pulsing here below, to dazzle our eyes and senses and the little port-resort acquired a new and alluring character, became transformed in our honour. Butterflies born in the sun flew about all the livelong day.

Betimes (secluded away together in those hidden places, in transports of joy in sea coves or lost in the bracken) my longing for the bitch was so intense, and never to be gratified, that my teeth ached. A drowsy numbness took hold of all my senses. I wanted to eat her; or, failing that, take a hatchet to her. I had a permanent hard-on, my hot imagination brought on promptings bad as that of the Aboriginal slavering away in the burning bush and frothing at the mouth. Or primitive men anywhere in the fastness of the world at any time, far worse than being afflicted with a hernia or severely ruptured; for 'well-hung' suggested nothing so much as freshly slaughtered game sizzling on a spit.

Philippa Phillips was my meat, all of her 63 kilos; all, all of a piece. My portion; we were made for each other, despite the discrepancy in age. Our prolonged gymnastics were necessarily restricted to an empty train carriage or a pine copse on the slopes of the Big Sugarloaf in winter; but in summer with all the freedom of out-of-doors we reverted to savages.

Could that be what Yeats – who himself came late to wedded bliss – had in mind when he wrote of 'The fury and the mire of human veins'? We know that the beasts of antiquity bred on the run, their glans encrusted with blood and excrement.

But a rendezvous after supper on the Greystones harbour wall was stretching it a bit. To watch the sunset! Not on your Nelly! Favours were favours, boons were boons; this was compromising.

I stood alone on the harbour wall to watch the red sun rise up out of the sea. Gulls were squabbling on the breakwater. Then a pack of scurvy eager mongrel dogs came trotting down to reconnoitre, to make an inspection, informally lifting a casual hind leg with ease born of long practice, to piss quickly on posts, car wheels, low walls, lamp-posts, sniffing the results, canine sprinklers getting the day going.

The familiar shrill whistle of the four o'clock train coming on the breeze announced her arrival. She was approaching me through all the tunnels as I waited by the station on my heavy Raleigh, right toecap to kerbside, and the piggy small hostile eyes of the obese Scuffle observed me from the hut.

She appeared suddenly and visionlike amid all the flustered

commuters pouring forth from the station.

Philippa Phillips stood out brown as a nut after a fortnight in Rome on Montessori business, dressed in a clinging summer frock with uplift bra. On her brown legs were Roman sandals laced up the calves to dimpled knee rears. She smelt of summery things, boxed tennis balls in mint condition because never used, cut fruit and freshly ironed cotton and linen. A difficult menses sometimes left her wan and bedraggled. She rarely if ever initiated moves but softly returned my ardently bold kisses in a slow hesitant manner with closed eyes, that drove me mad. On the night train we engaged in upside-down kissing against the grain of her pulpy lips, I playing the hard-hitting Donald Budge to her gentle Kay Stammers (this was before grunting became fashionable on the court). She returned my hard services ('you are lustier than I') with careful slow lobs of her own. My return smashes fairly took her breath away. Her own breath was always sweet. Do what you can; you learn as you go along.

Where from there? Well, first to tea with Mother; then with me into the bushes. No sooner out of sight than naked and clinging together in a long kiss, my manroot reversed, her hands defending her breasts, the large nipples already erected, brown as walnuts. And then the old refrain: 'No, no, we mustn't!'

She was a late arriver at life's feast, a middle child, the misunderstood one least loved, least favoured, leastways by her crotchety mother. Her old pater was already adrift into senility. The stern crewcut blond brother, Reverend Father Philip Phillips, SJ, was built like the young Gary Cooper, off converting heathens in some Ugandan mission station.

And Phil herself, what of her? She tried me sorely with her precepts and possibilities, her nays and her ayes ('Now you are being perfectly disgusting'). Her midwinter face was powdered chalk white as a Kabuki doll. Prim rosebud lips of Clara Bow, hands and feet most delicate and refined, a gentle musing voice — she did not question much; most things amused her — rounded limbs, rounded calligraphy, nut-brown hair rounded on curlers; modest scents, *contained* personal odours, nice airs and graces; her own shy stratagems to entrap and enslave. But no harbour wall, *if* you please.

Once and once only had we attempted and attained bunga-low bliss at Much Ado, the humble abode falling to bits, gaining surreptitious entrance to my tiny pink bedroom, like the interior of a mouth, hard by the kitchen sink. It had formerly been a lumber room or storage place for cleaning materials; by reaching out you could touch either wall from the centre of the cell. I had rigged up some bookshelves and there was my library, the Shakespeare, the Schopenhauers, the Huxley novels in uniform edition, *Antic Hay*, Burton's *Anatomy of Melancholy*.

Into this pink cell crept the three of us, the two of us and the dog, little Kurt. Philippa was undressed in a trice and had slipped between the clean aired sheets that I had taken from the line, doped with verbena, while Kurt with a contented deep sigh stretched himself out on the rug and industriously began to lick his prick, groaning and worrying as he trans-ferred his attention to his haunch and rump, gnawing after fleas, while I was after his mistress.

Brown as nougat Philippa lay obligingly on her stomach and I lay on top of her with my hard-on wrapped in woven white cotton bathing-drawers tied with a drawstring, serving as a primitive contraceptive device (since there were no balloons to hand, which in any event were forbidden). I cupped her crushed breasts in both my crossed hands, holding her secure, whispering soft words of appeasement, fastened my teeth into the odorous nape of her neck as a ferret might secure its victim, a rabbit stiff with fright and pinion it against the end-wall of the burrow, kill it with fright. Not that Philippa was in the least alarmed by this overt display of hairy male force.

In the ramshackle bathroom a defective cold tap dripped wastefully away. Shivering and groaning the dachshund watched what was going on in the bed, then sprang on to the coverlet and curled up at our feet, an heraldic beast, our

protector, while Philippa continued to whisper sweet
nothings into the pillow and I to pour semen while frantically
biting her neck, her short hair. I had mounted my rod, and
tried casting it shallow waters. If one starts drowning . . . if
you start drowning . . .

Suddenly we stopped drowning at Kurt's warning growl
deep in his stomach to alert us that someone was approaching.
And sure enough there came the sound of hard bicycle tyres
spurning the gravel and the yard door being yanked open
imperiously.

We heard the Dodo (for it was none other) hurl his
machine into the toolshed, then the kitchen door was rocked
to its hinges and rapid fussy footsteps oddly feminine tripped
across the buckled linoleum.

Making a face and naked as two plums, Philippa held the
little trembling beast tightly against her warm breasts to
quieten him, telling him to hush in a soft whisper, to hush up,
it was only the Dodo returning from his office in the city; at
which Kurt showed his fangs and bristled all along his spine,
like a hedgehog closing up.

Quietly and in orderly fashion we dressed and let ourselves
out the back way, softly through both doorways, on tippytoe
over the gravel, Philippa dishevelled, Rory affecting calm and
brave little Kurt vigorously wagging his tail in token of his
approval that we were away.

Badger, badger! Holt, holt! Hasten, hasten! Horn, horn!

Sometimes it was 'Sweetheart', sometimes it was 'Skunk';
but the King knew her not. Stardust and sinners' tears.

2

Sirius Rising

On moonless August nights in the dog days, with Sirius rising, in blossom time, in the happy blossom times, our bliss was complete. For then we had the whole of Kilcoole beach to ourselves and could cavort in our skins in the surf to our hearts' content, run from the dunes into the sea to kiss and embrace there, Philippa icy cold who a moment before had been roasting hot, splashing through the shallows as the tide flooded back in.

We swam through a phosphorescent sea that silvered her all over with gilded scales like a trout silvery and resplendent that I could ardently embrace, vigorously towel dry, she squirming, then eat her (her bush the garnishing), telling her she was my trout, my mare, I was both the poacher and the groom, the ostler whistling between his teeth, rubbing down the foddered mare Cabin Fire. I was rough Rod, up early to muck out the stables, groom the fidgety mare, curry-combing and plaiting, whoa there my beauty!

I'd lent her Herrick's bawdy love poetry to his mistress Julia ('On Going to the Bath' dog-eared for her attention), hoping to get her into the mood, but not at all, her susceptibilities were tender and tentative as the horns of a snail. I told her that her nipples were as 'strawberries half-drown'd in cream' when she wore white cotton. The bawdy verse of Dean Prior's Vicar was as water off a duck's back. Philippa considered 'Love perfumes all parts' in questionable taste. And what of it if he *had* taught his pig to sit with him in the garden and down his pint like a true-born gent, what was it to *her*? She was no great reader, this outsplashed lady, a siren sprung dripping from a canvas by Delacroix straight into my bed.

The incoming surf made soft sounds of systole and diastole like a sigh or series of small sighs one following the other to rattle the pebbles, running them in and out again, as if playing a game, before withdrawing with calm regularity in a sudden seething respiration on the shore. A wet cling, as in an embrace, the lips glued to other lips, the hand in the small of the back, then the parting exhalation, like a contented sigh.

Semen and seaweed smell of the nocturnal sea, the spumy splash and plash of the surf's inswell that hit us as we went in, in the nip, holding hands, Philippa quick to dip down, to hide her shame. We swam out together.

'I wonder if old Major Storey is watching us in the dark? Got his night-binoculars trained on us?'

In the moonlessness she emerged covered in gooseflesh, to be embraced and run along the shore, a white moth, a pale female shape drawn in light brown chalk on a blackboard, pounding along in her pelt. Night Stalker!

In the endless days of that phenomenally hot blue summer that burnt up the fairways of Delgany and Greystones we went in the nip in full sunshine on Kilcoole sands too hot to walk on with bare feet and ate cucumber sandwiches and fruit, sunbathing in the dunes hidden by seagrass, Pan and captive Nereid covered in pollen, gone the colour of autumn leaves. 'Make me come slowly. We have all day.'

It was none too easy to warm up that flesh of hers, to inflame a libido so placid and conforming; for the nuns had got to her and reformed her. That sweet smile on lips I had bruised was only a token acquiescence, deployed until the sticking point was reached, the hard chastity belt that she wore all the time under her clothes and even when stark naked, doing what she was not supposed to do, with tissues near. She had a core of unassailable virginity, wiping her hands. The order to stop, to disengage, was whispered hotly into my ear.

'Now you're being disgusting again!'

Stew me! What rash expenditure of spurting semen! She aroused me and made me randy as a billy-goat with her calm refusals, and how gladly would I have impregnated a whole screaming convent of randy hysterical pubescent schoolgirls, beginning with Mother Superior, blushing Sister Philippa with only rosary beads about her waist, fainting with desire. 'Get brutal with me, Rod lad.' Her long stint teaching with the nuns of Leeson Street had left her torpid in her fleshly appetites! Only her pious spirit gave a feeble glow; the rest was fallow ground.

I laid my hands on her bare whaddyoucallit, bit her, wantoned her, *gored* her.

'I'm sore. You made my breasts sore. You made them very sore, you beast you.'

'Sorry,' I mumbled in a beastly furtive way into my muffler, for it was winter, and we were hidden away in the firs on the slopes of the Small Sugarloaf on a bracingly cold day.

'What are you mumbling about now?'

'Nothing.'

'Horrid beast.'

'That's me. I'm your horrid beast.'

'You horrid thing!'

Her breasts were freckled like wrens' eggs, rarely seen and as hard to find; enhanced (when finally exposed) with large nipples the size of conkers.

Yet all that summer we had wrestled in the dunes, in the nip, in the sea, in the ferns, on the railway siding, on the embankment, I as eager to have what she was so purposeful to defend. We walked and sunbathed and dipped our inflamed parts in the chilly sea that made her nipples erect, as it caused my manroot to extend itself in an even more purposeful manner. I fingered her and she me, we came together. Who *mounts* the meek? (Quarles). What power is it, which *mounts* my loue so hye? (Shakes). My wiggywagtail.

Until I lay exhausted alongside her, failing to get inside her, the pair of us naked as salmon on the seashore, panting. Touch again her flesh, get her going, until I sapless, spent, lie by her. We were inseparable; she took it out of me (gingerly fishing my cock from my flies as if handling a viper become python).

Philippa's constant companion about Greystones was Kurt her little German sausage dog always trotting along briskly obedient at her heels. The elongated low-slung animal conveyed the impression, as do all that breed, of shameless canine nudity combined with shattered nerves. Kurt was indeed a nervous wreck; the collar and identity disc suggested S&M practices.

3

Stolen Kisses

She was shy as a postulant. The thick dark bush came as a great surprise, that hot hairy bun that she kept warm and secret between her legs, as the two smaller buns under both arms rounded as one of Tiepolo's androgynous angels (did I detect a whiff of incense?). Philippa was full of Mother Nature's feminine juices, fairly brimming over. I counterfeited a proper Romantic anguish and laid hold of her, stuttering my importunity: 'Oh I have such desyre to know thee, Philippa! To know thee carnally!'

'You may kiss the small of my back,' she said primly.

My urgent and pressing adoration required much strenuous outdoor bussing and fondling even in winter frost and snow and in the remotest places (the remoter the better because there I could go further), between the railway tunnels, on the side of the Big Sugarloaf. We hiked to Greystones from Bray and from Bray to Greystones by the cliff walk to see old movies at the Roxy and Royal and Stanley Illsley and Leo McCabe in plays by Giradoux and Wilde and walked home in the moonlight to dip in the nip in Greystones harbour or by the culvert on the south beach away from the huddled forms of Major Storey and his wife, inveterate night-fishers on their camp-stools, and Philippa phosphorescent in the spumy spray whispered 'You are lustier than I.'

4

Philippa's Aged Parents

Philippa's parents were old as the hills.

To a quite marvellous degree old Paul Phillips resembled the Boer War hero General Jan Smuts. Same goatee beard, stiff cravat and look of unflinching rectitude. They were dead ringers. Stiff too and forbidding in manner and mien was old Mrs Paula Phillips, an elderly lady of dignified demeanour all powdered up to sally out, impress the neighbours with her edifying example. She had made it plain that she disapproved of me laying siege to her elder daughter. Threw me a leery look.

Moving at a slow and stately pace she made her way around the corner into Trafalgar Road and so over the footbridge – humpbacked as so many things in Greystones, the seaside resort where Protestants come to die – spanning the railway line and thus to the church for evening devotions. She was somewhat humpbacked herself, stricken by the years.

Muffled up in monkbrown bombazine with a veiled pothat impaled with an eight-inch hat-pin on her haughty head of old hair pulled tight in a bun, on her feet buttoned boots from a previous era, a plaid shawl draped about her bulky shoulders, she carried a short furled umbrella with amber holder, a prayer book in the other gloved hand; and so accoutred advanced puffing and panting and prodding the footpath in an ill-tempered way with the savagely pointed

ferrule. Crossly she advanced, ruffling her drab feathers, a
Rhode Island Red unable to settle before a dust-bath, to calm
her nerves. She had a hen pheasant's eye.

She was a restless religious discontented woman and
nothing in the world could please her. I could detect no trace
of Philippa in her except perhaps a certain disdainful twitch of
the nostril, sometimes.

5

The Bouncing Balls

The Ball brothers were well oiled as ball-bearings; they liked a drop. Having lost a leg on Anzio Beach Captain Andy limped for the rest of his life, until lost without trace with the crew of the ill-fated *Joyita* in the fastness of the Tasman Sea. The little ketch had been found a month later a thousand miles off course with a shelter arranged aft as if a solitary survivor had hung on there until provisions gave out and he slipped over the side to join his companions in Davy Jones's locker where an unkind fate had sent them months before.

'Knocked on the head by savages,' Brandy drawled through dense fumes of Three Nuns. 'Or maybe eaten by cannibals.' Hahahahaha!

Many's the time I'd partnered or opposed battling Captain Andy in singles and friendly fourballs about County Wicklow and Dublin from the Grange to Portmarnock. He reeking of Bushmills, chain-smoking, stumping fiercely off the first tee at ten in the morning and out onto the dewy fairway.

Once in a mixed foursome with Ena Wilkinson and prim and proper Dolly Oulton, Brandy was passing water in one of the corrugated iron shelters with foreskin retracted when he was stung painfully by a nettle, on his cock. Andy split himself laughing.

The British Army officer and hero of Anzio (DSO and bar)

stumped about on one artificial leg, listing to port and starboard, too proud to use a stick, pickled in excellent Scotch and perspiring profusely.

Both brothers sweated heavily, oozing alcohol from every pore. Brandy kept one stabilising elbow on the bar counter, wiping his overheated brow with Kleenex, ever anon relapsing into sudden storms of coughing that bent him double, purple in the face, giving the death-rattle of a smoker's cough to end them all. The clubhouse wet-wit Joe Mulderry declared that it was Brandy who deserved the bar, whatever about the gong. The male members guffawed and slapped him on the back while Captain Ball smiled a bleak smile. Hor-horr-hor! They were a mouthy lot, proud of their club wit, such as it was, the dopey idiom of village gossip.

Mulderry was Managing Director of Polikoff Rainwear and drank like a fish, could probably have drunk the two Balls under the table, for he was truly pickled in strong spirits and drank all the time; whereas Brandy had to remain sober some of the time, in order to manage his boot factory with any degree of competence.

Capillary vessels had erupted and burst in Brandy's blazing cheeks now gone purple, like so many drunken asteroids in the night sky, a kind of alcoholic fireworks display. He had the snouted appearance of a hedgehog, the snubby nose with delicate nostrils, damp nostril hair showing when he struggled with his pipe; the little bloodshot eyes dark as sloes, with an oily, shifty sheen that was the booze speaking.

He stumbled about in his rubberyblubbery way, as if on convex soles, topsy-turvy as a spinning top running down, beginning to keel over. Heavy intakes of alcohol had made him the way he was, uncertain on his pins (locomotor ataxy), freighted down with gallons of Dutch lager, his morning tipple to get him going, then quarts and firkins of good-quality wine and spirits to get through the day and lighten the evening and night, propping up the bar in storms of coughing, four or more sheets into the wind when he knew he had had enough at last, stumbling hastily from the bar. Then the slam of the car door below, the engine racing, accelerating off over the cattle trap, and as like as not ending up in Lewis's or the Clyda ('One for the road!'). The Guards (Charley Reynolds) turned a blind eye; licensing hours were flexible, serious drinkers could be accommodated as long as they gave no trouble, and the brothers Ball were a victualler's delight. Brandy was regarded with affection by all who knew him. He was a card.

Mellowed by prodigious daily intake of spirits Joe Mulderry had the yellowed complexion of a wizened mummy long put away into some dusty catafalque; doubtless the internal cells had atrophied, kidneys and lungs in dire straits.

6

The Undertaker of Aungier Street

Wilmot Wilkinson, he of the twisted lip and the florid complexion (florid as behoves an undertaker, an onerous and dirty job, like refuse collection, that has to be done) was on fire with copious libations of Bell's whisky and loaded down with all the sour accumulated grief of the day that had slowly seeped into his very soul. And an undertaker's soul must indeed be a grief-sodden one, for his working days are endless, he trades in grief, does business with the recently bereaved, the widow-of-a-day, the wifeless husband; they take their toll. Morticians only become drunkards out of sympathy for their suffering clients.

Coming home on the last train, much the worse for wear (what with Bell's and hand-wringing and apt condolences) to solace his sadness he sometimes picked up stray sluts parading along the damp platform at Bray station and shagged them silly all the way through the tunnels. For a few quid they obliged – working-class girls with easy morals, smelling high as badgers in their setts.

He emerged dramatically and drunkenly from a first-class non-smoker, unsteady on his pins, speechless and footless, hitting the open gate with his shoulder and falling.

Risen again, helped to his feet like a boxer in the ring, he made off into the dark, staggering away down the sea road, much to the amusement of Willie Doyle the ticket collector

20

who was keeping an eye on the slut now slinking to the ticket office for a single return to Bray, the final run back to the terminus, a fiver richer.

Sometimes aboard too would be the coldly sober un-frocked clergyman whose mind, greatly disturbed, was a teeming riot of filthy images and leaping devils going about their business of torturing souls. He had rodent teeth brown to the roots and a fund of filthy stories which he liked to void into the appalled ears of single women travelling alone, frightening them out of their wits, his vile breath steaming forth as out came the filth. For him it was perhaps a form of confession that included absolution. Maybe it gave him some relief, like a stiff smelly stool.

7

On Being Whirled Away

With her customary caution Philippa deplored all 'underhand dealings' and 'backstairs intrigues'; she was one of life's late arrivals. Her movements were both shy and seductive; very composed, she had a pale face. Pimply Prudence, her plain sister, spitefully called Philippa 'Lardy-Face', whereas it was *she* who had the lardy face. She was jealous of our happiness, if it was happiness; for Philippa was my troubled love, as all first love must be.

Philippa had a prudish little o for a mouth but a voluptuous body; the games mistress transformed under the shower, steaming.

In the morning sun the larks sang as they spiralled up from their nests in the ripening wheat and we sunbathed in the nip behind cement blocks that made a sea wall at the point of the south beach where the little stream flowed out.

In the evening sun on the slope of the wheatfield she confessed – and how much it must have cost her! – that in the event of the old love ever returning, she would have to drop me 'like a hot brick'.

I knew whom she would drop me in favour of, I knew whom she meant, having seen them going out together. He came before me. Oft had they canoodled in the back row of the balcony at the Ormonde Cinema. With his false teeth removed the false poltroon protested that he felt ashamed to kiss her; but she said that she didn't mind, he should go ahead and give her a kiss. So he clamped himself on to her and gave her a long clinging, lingering slobbery loathsome toothless *kuss*, the rascally Kraut, so he did.

Where?

In the back row of the balcony.

Who?

Kurt Klingsore.

But who is this Beau Brummel, this hole-and-corner upstart, this balcony groper? tell me, tell me. None other than Klingsore whose rolypoly sister Ena is the wife to the lean mildewed Wilkinson, the man with the twisted lip (from rather close shaves), undertaker of Aungier Street where it always rains; it just pours down on the mourners assembled there.

Well, I did not exactly whirl her off her feet. I had no money (a great want); was I not poor, lived from hand to mouth on handouts, like Murphy. But the quiet fishing village cum seaside resort had become transformed into a little paradise fit for us. The space occupied by PP, where she lived and breathed, whirled me away. She simply whirled me away. Or was it love that whirled me off?

Mind you, she was no raging beauty, no *femme fatale*, a handmaiden in the Great Court of Love, at which she was an indifferent participant. Yet she was not my type, that's possible.

Though virgo intacta she had the body of a breeder. Breedy breasts and wiggywagtail bum, with her mother's suspicious eye in the undergrowth. *She* would have had kittens had she seen rough Rod the cocky groom run alongside her daughter and the pair without a stitch on them and Rod with Bronze Age erection that only grew stronger with running and air and total immersion in the iodiny sea. Rod wanted to stick it up her accommodatingly big bum.

But oh dear me no, she just couldn't oblige (her priest had extracted a promise). No, not her; oh she just couldn't, not after confession, in the summertime, in the summertime, in the glimmer time, on the harbour wall.

She was somewhat pigeon-toed, or perhaps it was knock-kneed, depending how you look at it; it gave her a hip sway, a nautical swagger. I found the in-turn, the dimpled backs of the knees, the sway, very attractive, it suggested a sort of fainting submission to a sufficiently brutal approach. She was certainly a bit of a flirt. It was all part of her brown-skinned charm. She wore summer dresses cut straight across the bust, with her arms and back bare; on request offered me un-depilated armpits to lingeringly kiss and would obligingly raise her skirt or lower her panties in semi-retreats (overlooking the White Rock, overlooking the railway line beyond the tunnel) to expose her all so that I might fondle her.

'I desire you, Philippa.'

'If we were married you could have me every morning like porridge.'

'Maybe I don't like porridge.'

'Then I'd be your All-Bran, your Wheat Flakes.'

Her defensive strokes were immaculate, her strategy hard to disarm.

'Do me up the back, lovey. Zip me up.'

Only the terns and mews that laid their eggs on the beach and circled screeching over Philippa's head as she went in her pelt into the sea knew what was going on in the dunes, between dips, on our private nudist beach at Kilcoole. Peeping Toms crept along the path on hands and knees, hunkering up to take a quick dekko (heraldic beasts extending dexter paws) and then softly down again, gliding along the sandy path like snakes, like eels, like lugworms. Or, upright, strolling by, whistling to indicate innocence of intent, or standing stock still, appraising horizon in a rapt and studied fashion, as if no impure thought had ever crossed their filthy minds.

Apart from these annoyances we had the beach to ourselves (Major Storey and wife as blurs in the distance in the heat haze, indistinguishable from the cement blocks that guarded the railway line), to eat our tomato sandwiches and Marmite, fruit, Cadbury, in peace. On good days her flesh was on fire.

Philippa was brown as one of Gauguin's odalisques, brown all over but for the soles of her feet and the palms of her hands. Once by a reservoir near Lucan a fox had broken cover to trot down and drink, observing us craftily from the far bank, its muzzle in the water, observing Philippa tearing off her panties, Edwige Feullière succumbing. 'I'd be your slave and doormat.'

As a girl she had gone roller-skating at the Bray rink and noticed a tall self-possessed youth who was Garrett Fitzgerald home from boarding school.

Once as a grown girl with drink taken, in puce ballgown and imitation pearls, she had shimmied up the long drapes of the ballroom of the Grand Hotel in Greystones to touch the pelmet with her fingertips and slide down to the applause of dancers hardly less sober than she.

I accompanied her up in the little elevator cage at Brown Thomas above the ladies' lingerie department, to change her mother's lending library book on the first floor.

Below us the metal canisters conveying small change flew back and forth along their wires, crashed into the sockets. They were packed with silver and coppers like Mills bombs or hand grenades.

Once a month in winter I took a bath at the Railway Hotel (our cold tap ran summer and winter but we had no hot water) opposite the station for sixpence, cycling there with a bath-cube in my pocket for a shampoo that left my hair stiff and matted as the dusty coat of a Kerry Blue.

Josey the golfing barber cut my hair, demonstrating Jimmy Bruen's peculiar golf swing ('a swing within a swing') in his emporium near Scuffle's hut. He cut my hair for two bob with the same clippers used on corpses whom he laid out neat for interment.

From the stoutly perspiring Scuffle I bought a No. 2 wood known as a brassie in those days. I paid him £2 and kept it for years. Until I sold my clubs and took the mailboat to England.

8

The Grafton Picture House
and Restaurant

All was different then. A courteous time of 'dating' and 'walking out' together and a courting that meant darting forward to open doors or pull back chairs for ladies. Such Hollywood-inspired gallantries were commonplace in the days when bikes (not to mention daughters) could be left unguarded and unchained against area railings.

It was all Pond's face cream and powder puffs for pretty girls in chiffon and womanly women in starched taffeta.

'I knew you fancied me by the way you stared at my lips.'

'Oh any excuse.'

Philippa wore a bison brown velveteen overcoat with a dotey sprig of something scented in the lapel and a sort of cowl or hood about which she draped her Switzer's silk scarf, a fashion borrowed from Maureen O'Hara in *Sitting Pretty* where she was the very prim and proper American housewife wedded to Robert Young, a hubby much given to pipe-drill and quizzical looks, a coy little smirk playing about the corners of his curly lips.

We saw Deborah Kerr and Robert Donat (ever looking ill) as drab wife and dispirited city clerk with a permanent cold sitting silently at breakfast, gazing with loathing at his soft-boiled egg in *Perfect Strangers*; the drab couple who later are transformed by war and become gallant, he in the Royal Navy and she in the WAAFS, coming together at the end. In the balcony of the Capital with all its ornate boxes I felt Philippa melting, her overcoat slipped back on the seat and the place warm as a sauna with its cigarette fumes and body heat.

Old Paul Phillips rustled the pages of the *Irish Times* at old Mrs Phillips who was turning the pages of the *Catholic Standard* and wondering what her eldest daughter was getting up to with her young Catholic suitor, a most unsuitable match, she felt, eructating, wheezy, troubled with indigestion.

We walked out together to the tune of 'These Foolish Things'. We were teamed up in the mixed fourballs at the Greystones Golf Club; as members of the Irish Film Society we sat in the balcony of the De Luxe in Camden Street and saw Edwige Feuillère in *Le Blé en herbe* at a Saturday matinée. Philippa was in the Ladies, applying powder and lipstick, freshening up for nice tea at the Grafton Restaurant upstairs. For she knew that the bold Rory would eat her up in a first-class non-smoker all the way to Greystones through the tunnels, if we had a carriage to ourselves, as private as a closed *fiacre* to the Bois.

We walked through the Green to Grafton Street and mounted the steps of No. 72, a mock Elizabethan edifice that stood opposite Harris's music shop with mouth organs and mandolins on display in the window with squeeze-boxes like cash registers arranged on their sides on purple baize.

An elderly retainer with frizzy grey hair twinkled out at us, squeezed tightly into the ticket office that was cramped as a confessional and made of the same sombre dark wood suggestive of penitence. *South Riding* was showing. We ascended the carpeted stairs and into the lovely eating emporium above the vestibule where I helped to remove her overcoat and scarf and hung them on the wooden rack. By the faint illuminations of the little table lamps with maroon shades and tassels Philippa studied the menu.

One who had come there often to eat in the 1940s has described it well: 'Its bill of fare [is] hallowed in one's memory. Consisting totally as it did of variations under a theme of different names, all nearly amounting to exactly the same thing.'

Why, he could have been describing our cavorting by the shore and tumbles in the hay, more properly speaking, bracken. The menu of the day went unchanged down the years, offering:

> Tasty Tea, Evening Tea,
> Tempting Tea, Afternoon Tea,
> Savoury Tea, Snack Tea and (in awestruck italics)
> The Gourmet's Tea.

'Will you chance the tempting tea?' I suggested lecherously, pressing her foot. Thoughtful Philippa bit her lip. An anchovy on a slice of toast was added to whatever you had with the others; but this exotic fare was reserved for gourmets only.

> The sombrely illuminated room [wrote the traveller in time], its tall-ceilinged interior resembled the galleried hall of a great country house [in Westmeath, perchance?]. There was a screen in a darkened corner behind which an elevator brought food up from the kitchen below. Upholstered chairs and banquettes upon which to sit under the lofted imitation beamed ceiling. The recessed wide sills of the fake Tudor windows and mock mahogany furnishings.

The waitresses were up from the country and emerged slowly from behind the screen to hover over our table, pencil and pad poised to take the order. It was like a picnic in a wood, served by dryads.

'Oh I'll just have the usual,' I said airily.

The traveller ends: 'Such was the solemnity of this place's marvellous strange peace.'*

The toilets were situated in the basement below the vestibule. Between Ladies and Gents hung a bizarre man-

* J. P. Donleavy, Ireland in All Her Sins and Some of Her Graces.

sized poster blue-tinged as with leprosy showing Doukhobors or Okies cowering under great storm clouds that tower up above the dry prairies. An enigmatic caption read: SOON IT WILL BE THEIR TURN.

I stood at the urinal and marvelled as pedestrians carrying parcels walked above my head; the soles of their shoes pressed down on the rhomboids of thick glass and up above there was a whisper of rain.

9

An Aged Barber

It was when *The Best Years of Our Lives* was running for ever and ever in the musty old Metropole and Sean O'Faolain, editor of the *Bell*, was demanding bananas on his breakfast cereal and the war was on. I was seated in a barber's chair in an underground emporium in O'Connell Street near Nelson's Pillar where the trams started for Dalkey and Palmerston Park from the heart of the Hibernian metropolis. You could get a short back and sides for two bob with a sixpenny tip thrown in. Maison Prost on Stephen's Green and Suffolk Street were the posh places where you paid more.

My mother used to say that barbers were like slugs, they led such unnatural lives. The old one who was clipping my hair would have been born around 1870; now with bad halitosis and fallen arches, moving slowly, wearing the white smock favoured by barbers and dentists. He had behind him a long unhealthy underground working life in electric light with never enough exercise or fresh air in the People's Gardens in the Phoenix Park, putting in long hours for poor remuneration, always on his feet, in the days when trams still ran and the elevated Bovril sign was spilling its stupendous cinnabar neon gules all over College Green.

The old barber was clipping my neck and blowing the hairs away and wheezing into my ear some pleasantries about one of his more famous clients who had come puffing down the narrow wooden steps off the street, as I had. A broad fat man in an Inverness cape, with a cane and a wide-brim black hat, and quizzing-glasses depending from a stylish black cord. The Gargantuan subsidence of elephantine buttocks supporting the vast bulk of the great public debater who had disputed matters of moment with Shaw and Belloc, written *The Man Who Was Thursday* and the Father Brown stories, almost put paid to the barber's chair. Some years before, he (G. K. Chesterton) had monumentally occupied the very seat on which I sat being tickled by short hairs down my collar.

One fine May morning I was walking west along Waterloo Road when whom should I see approaching on the same pavement but a small-sized, brown-faced man in a pale serge suit and tan brogues, hatless, a miniature lariat serving for a tie, that gave him a look of Hopalong Cassidy. He glanced at me as he passed by. It was Frank O'Connor.

Years in the States had imparted a Yankee swagger to Mr O'Donovan, formerly of Cork City, who wrote for *Holiday* magazine and the *New Yorker* under the pseudonym of Frank O'Connor, whose early work my mother had venerated – *The Saint and Mary Kate*.

One grey onyx-and-opal day so typical of Dublin weather, I was waiting to book a ticket for *Winterset* which was about to open at the Gaiety Theatre with Burgess Meredith and Paulette Goddard, when the very lady, Chaplin's leading lady, passed through by the stage entrance, with a sweet smile for the waiting punters, and for me.

Alistair Cooke was writing a script for Chaplin as Napoleon in exile on St Helena, working on Chaplin's yacht, and watched Paulette Goddard in a bathing costume; he said she looked 'trim and shiny as a trout'.

On the stage for the Maxwell Anderson play she brought a touch of glamour, a suggestion of an exotic world outside Dublin and the musty drapes and the safety curtain with old advertisements for Virol and Eno's Fruit Salts.

It was a time when I yearned to get out of Ireland but lacked the neck, the gall, the courage to walk up the gang-plank of one of those foreign vessels tied up along the quays near Butt Bridge. Famous ones had passed through, trailing clouds of glory. And I was stuck there.

Oh, clay.

10

The Old Flame on Butt Bridge

Years roll by, as roll they must.

One grey Dublin day didn't I find myself back, twenty-five years on and now the father of three bouncing boys, passing over Butt Bridge (itself strangely deserted) when who should appear out of the nowhere abracadabrawise but a familiar famished face and form dressed more or less as before who made as if to walk past me without a nod or smile of greeting nor any sign of recognition whatsoever: the Old Flame!

She cast a look of sour aspersion in my direction as if to dismiss me, a low fellow trying to trick her, pick her up on the middle of Butt Bridge; she hurrying on, outraged honour engraved in every quick motion of her rump.

'Phil! What's got into you? Don't you remember me? Rory.' This drew her up short; adrift and at a loss (was there even a suggestion of widow's peak?); halted in her tracks but conveying the impression of hurrying away at top speed. Ah but those shy subterfuges still scalded my heart. I had heard that she had married G. F. B. Ball, 'Brandy' to his intimates, former Captain and then Vice-President of the golf club where Philippa was Lady Captain. Brandy owned a footwear factory in Athlone; he had died of the drink, leaving most of his money to a sister in Taunton.

And still we were meeting on bridges; for had not our very

first rendezvous been on the little humpbacked bridge over the duckpond in Stephen's Green one greyly overcast day like this one, when she had come strolling to meet me there?

Who said that first love has this in common with last love, it is again involuntary? What aches a man is go back to what he remembers, wrote Faulkner. As you taste it you destroy it, say the wine buffs.

'When he performs all joy deserts him,' Ernest Ansermet mocked the anxious Stravinsky on the podium, conducting a performance of one of his own works that he knew by heart but was unable to take his eyes off the score. Nervous as a child on the first day at school, Stravinsky had pushed his music stand up against the rail in order to count time.

At my entreaty she advanced starkers into the dark waters of Lough Dan, thought to be bottomless. The mountain lake engulfed her as she cautiously advanced to be dismembered inchmeal; legs first to go, then the hips and mound of Venus, the dimpled rump and cleft, then the belly and bust (all centre and no circumference, as Celia's); until all of her was severed up to the neck and only the poor flustered face floated free on the dark unruffled surface of the lake (the sun having retreated behind a cloud and the lake become darker). The face still smiled bravely back at me as the water closed about her neck. 'It's warm as toast in!' inanely sang out the decapitated head afloat on the darkening surface, as she launched herself and began a ladylike circumspect breaststroke out into the lake.

'I'm coming!' I called, dropping my trousers.

Closing my eyes and drawing a deep breath in I went after her and struck out bravely for the further shore.

Istanbul, anyone? Who's for Venezuela? Buenos Aires? Montevideo? All the seas of the world.

PART II:

No. 11
Springhill Park

Preamble

> Time . . . attenuates memories.
> Byron, *Journal*

My father is in an old people's home down the way.
He pisses his pants like Molloy, grumbles like
Malone, crouches over the electric fire (two bars),
sets his pants on fire, burns pills in the grate. The birds sing.
Spring is under way.

The doctor gives him a week or two. He just about holds on,
mind almost gone. Now they call it cancer. He would be in pain
but for the drugs. He has your letter but probably doesn't
understand it & will hardly reply. The operation caused the
symptoms to spread all over, & to the mind. Person & events
have become confused & interchangeable for him. He says you
were fitted with false teeth when you were here but lost them,
& himself and Jimmy Martin looked for them but didn't find
them. He told me he was taking the boat. Next day he said he
slept it out. He gets up at night & tries to get out the window
etc. & is a danger to himself & others. In Duns they would cage
him in bed. His paranoia & aggressiveness increase with his
helplessness.

A letter from my brother.

37

11

My Father Dies

A third of our life-span is spent in sleep. Two-thirds of the Earth's surface lies underwater, as three-fourths of Connemara lies less than a hundred feet above sea level; so a good third of one's address book contains addresses of friends gone to another country, ex-friends, suicides, dead friends (the truest) gone to the other country from whence none return.

In Ireland we are always walking into the past. Even a thoroughly flat country such as County Kildare, my home county, opens willy-nilly into the past. A curious past without Renaissance or Reformation, without flag or proper government, without national identity or street lighting, without an effective police force until Sir William Peel in 1822 introduced the peelers.

It was a dark hole then.

The laws had not yet been committed to writing; there were no written records until the seventh or eighth century. 'Thus separated from the rest of the known world and in some way to be distinguished as another world,' famously declared King Henry II's amanuensis and historian, Giraldus Cambrensis, the wily Welsh fox.

The Dutch historian Huizinga considered his work to be a kind of poetry, a kind of dreaming; historical understanding would be akin to a vision. He compared the wigs of English judges in capital punishment days to the dancing masks of savages; for when they donned the death-cap it performed a similar function: transformed the wearer into another being. He wrote: 'There is not a more dangerous tendency in history than that of representing the past as if it were a rational whole, dictated by clearly defined interests.'

Stoutly argued, Dutchman, but where does it leave the poor mealy-mouthed Irish? Still in the lurch? Cromwell put his black curse on us. He wanted to drive the entire race back to their primitive origins, have them crawl about on hands and knees on the foreshore of Kilkieran Bay, become seal-hunters and scavengers living just above subsistence level, revert to savages, barking mad.

I saw a scarecrow striding manfully downhill by the Dargle stream in County Wicklow near the Mulcahys' summer retreat. Pheasants are calling in a piny wood and cattle with dungy hindquarters slowly wending their way, without herdsman or dog to direct them, towards the byre. A little boy lost or being punished weeps bitterly by the rainy outskirts of Rathdrum.

In days gone by a man would sometimes allow his horse to choose the way. No more; now no horse, no way. (Just going for a ramble threw Johan Huizinga into a kind of trance; he did his thinking while walking.)

History?

Pâté de foie gras stuffed with rat poison, a servant sharpening knives, a shout in the street. Albert Speer locked away for twenty long years and three fat keys turned thrice – for Spandau Prison is within Berlin, and Berlin was within the Wall, a hundred miles inside the GDR – noted in his secret diary a thought from Henry James: 'Next to great joy, no state of mind is so frolicsome as great distress.' And amended this rather finely with: 'There are situations in which fear and hope become one, mutually cancel each other out and are lost in the dark absence of being': (*Verloren im Dunkel der Seinsferne*). Speer knew whereof he spake. The real city lies all about him but he cannot see it, any more than its strolling citizens can see him, nor Hess, nor Baldur von Schirach; all three must serve out their sentences, but Hess will never be released.

One day in the sixteenth year of his long sentence he had a brief opportunity to furtively embrace his wife, but he did not avail himself and let the chance slip; fearing, if caught, to get some of his guards in trouble; or else himself troubled and his will weakened by penal years gone and others yet to be undergone. He didn't do it; didn't stir.

To retain his sanity he undertakes immensely long imaginary walks.

Crossing the Spandau exercise yard with Rudolf Hess, who may be mad, he hears a cock crowing over the wall in the city, and the exultant cries of excited children at play. He walks across the garden he has planted, uprooted by the Russians every third month, walks on right out of Spandau prison, out of Berlin, over the Wall, walks through the DDR like a man sleepwalking, walks out of Germany, out of Europe, crosses the Bering Strait as evening falls. In time he has traversed a distance equal to the perimeter of the Earth itself, finds himself in Kars, in Turkey, as night falls. He has been there before, on his holidays, he knows the place. Now on the slopes of a mountain a tent has been pitched, a lantern swings from a pole, two figures sit peacefully by the fire, himself and a guard. Above their heads hums the immense firmament blazing with stars. Will he always have a guard as his constant companion?

A lawnmower is being pulled and pushed back and forth through scutch grass behind the Balcony in Killiney, a house rented by the painter Harper and his Yorkshire wife Pat. I heard it one misty morning as I climbed Killiney Hill. A mile off, over another hill, my father was dying of cancer.

With a sudden squealing of brakes a red single-decker bus (No. 59) makes a tight left by the Sylvan Café. Someone has painted in big white emphatic capitals on the wall:

NO!

A fog of freezing air blows dust and papers by Regan's pub and in the airless lounge a tall Mayoman with incipient jigs raises a double brandy to his rubbery lips, twisting his mouth to ingest the draught as though swallowing cyanide at eleven o'clock in the morning.

Out of the clinging mist that swallowed up Dalkey Island in a trice comes a donkey pulling a trap carrying tinkers and their possessions, redheaded children hanging on for dear life, the angry father standing and hurling abuse at the little fast-trotting donkey and lashing at its spine.

They sweep past Regan's, a blur of nomadic faces seen for a moment before vanishing down the hill. The pub in Killiney, the only one, is called the Druid's Chair. My father informs me that in the olden times it was the headquarters of a convention of Druids.

I enter the park, look down into the seaweed beds. Behind the Druid's Chair a white horse stands fetlock-deep in lush grass with a jackdaw perched on its back. Young Mrs Harper in scarlet hot-pants strolls along the footpaths under hawthorn and cherry, a figure in a Pre-Raphaelite painting. Down a step in a shabby snug in Dalkey village a betting man circles his fancy with a ballpoint on the list of the afternoon runners at Leopardstown. He has put a few bob on Royal Braide.

The dense white mist, thick as cotton wool, rolled in from Dublin Bay and covered Dalkey Island. A lone blackbird sings in the clinging mist below the obelisk: *Aujour d'hui! Aujourd'hui!'*

In the seventy-eighth year of his life my father is dying of cancer. The surgery has been too much for him. He shuffles forward as if on snow-shoes, stopping frequently. He might as well be on crutches; it would be something else to complain about, take his mind off himself.

'It isn't right, Rory. It's not *right*. I can hardly walk. Never thought it would come to this.' A shake of the head, and he shuffles forward, stops again. I beg a lift of a passing motorist and we are conveyed down in style to Fitzgerald's.

My old man had been a keen horseman in his day, golfer, breeder of greyhounds, a backer of horses, a dreamer of winners (for a whole month in the Burnaby he had dreamed winners, almost broke the local bookie, who had never known such rank outsiders come romping home at such long odds), a rider of women, too, by all accounts; or so he liked to imply.

He holds a hot toddy in both hands, warming them, and stares at me with his vapoury duck-egg blue eyes. 'Do you tell me so now?'

Above the low lintel of the sunken Gents a notice is tacked up: MIND YOUR HEAD. My fingers tingle. The face in the mirror looks strange. In monstrous mime it (the face not mine) conveys the message: *One day you too will be old and helpless as he. And how will you like that, Mister*? Eh?

The Earth pulls towards it all falling bodies. The Gnostics believed that the angels put the same question to every dead person: 'Where do you come from?'

My father was dying piecemeal. His wandering mind couldn't hold on to any subject: they slipped from his grasp. His thoughts wandered about in vaguely concentric circles, loosely adrift like clouds. Choice seemed both endless and tiresomely circumscribed.

At No. 11 Springhill Park in Killiney a goldfish tank of unclean water turning toxic stands at the stairhead leading to my father's cramped and chintzy room. At the bottom of the tank a dying goldfish lies upside down with its intestines hanging out. My old man's mind is elsewhere, fretfully mulling over the extinct past and its retinue of cronies long gone but still gabby and full of gassy life, going on with their stories, in my father's mind. He has not much strength left in him, extending both hands to the red glow of the electric fire pulled close to his chair. His fingers open and close, taking in the heat, a cat feeling the fires.

Sometimes he, the ever-extravagant one, the big spender, chooses to forget that he is destitute, on the dole, asks to be booked into a hotel or into hospital; anywhere away from the regime of Mrs Hill, the ex-nurse who runs the place, referred to as 'that Presbyterian bitch'.

He examines the contents of his pockets, bulging with letters and newspaper clippings, stubs from the Malta Sweepstakes. His liquids have been severely cut down, alcohol is not permitted on these premises. In the toilet he kneels before the flushing bowl, dips in his cupped hands and drinks. I had brought him a noggin of John Jameson and this we must drink with him, he insists. Always and ever the big spender, the good fellow, the buyer of rounds. He hides the bottle under his pillow with other contraband, putting one over on the officious bitch.

When he leaves the room she will come poking around, making up the bed, fluffing out the pillow, emptying the pisspot, throwing open the windows, confiscating the whiskey.

The old ones assemble below in an airless livingroom, pick over the magazines long out of date, gape at the TV, doze off, passing the time until another square meal comes around again. A stale spent smell permeates this establishment presided over by the ruddyfaced and brusque former nurse, Mrs Hill. She encourages the feeble old ones to take some fresh air; the gardens of Killiney are in their gorgeous May bloom. And why not take advantage of it?

As my wife and I were leaving she stopped us at the foot of the stairs. 'Have any – mmm – arrangements been made?'

I was shocked as by blasphemy or an obscenity; but the ex-nurse knew her job and had read the signs correctly: my old fellow wasn't long for this world. He would die alone amid strangers, making jokes, joshing, letting them know that he was a great man once.

No such arrangements had been made, no coffin ordered, no grave plot booked. Dr Duffy the kidney expert was in sporadic attendance. With close-cropped fair hair and manicured fingernails Dr Duffy halted at the top of the stairs, with his fingernails taps the tank of now greenish stagnant water and the sick goldfish stirs, turns over slowly, giddily dying.

'Hmmm,' Dr Duffy murmured to himself and passed downstairs with his medical bag in hand.

'Evening, Doctor. Grand day.'

'Evening, Mrs Hill. It is indeed.'

Everything was in apple-pie order at No. 11 Springhill Park.

12

57 Beskidenstrasse

On 27 May 1969, a bright sunny day with wind (Watt's weather) in Dublin Airport, a perfect day for flying, said my wife (our middle lad James got sick all over the expensive Hollywood tan brogues of Mel Ferrer, immersed in the *Irish Press*), and we all boarded an Aer Lingus flight for Heathrow where we would join a Lufthansa flight to Berlin Tempelhof.

A swinishly stout German couple pushed their way to the head of the queue. We descended through thin cloud at Bremen, thicker cloud at Hanover, and touched down from a clear blue sky at Berlin Tempelhof at 1400 hrs, where Peter Nestler's own secretary, Fräulein Barbara Weschler (in thick pebble spectacles) awaited us, holding aloft a banner with this strange device:

PROFESSOR O'HILLS, WE ARE DAAD!

We had arrived; another life had begun. The Berlin air was effervescent and smelt of pine, *everybody* spoke German, Fräulein Weschler simply could not do enough for us, she was ours to command. Herr Nestler's big car would be at our disposal, and he himself would drive us around. The right house would be found for Herr Professor O'Hills and his lovely Frau and grand kids.

After a month of searching, a fine mansion was indeed

found in Beskidenstrasse in nookshotten Nikolassee near Krumme Lanke.

Zbigniew Herbert from Poland, seldom sober, lived with his titled wife at the far end of the long tree-lined road. Mando Arravintinou from Greece was over at Wildpfad. We were amid the more distinguished DaaD *Gäste* in Berlin.

The wooded surroundings were full of squirrels, strange birds made their calls at night, the Havel lakes were near. In Krumme Lanke French divers searched the Oxo-dark lake bed for wreckage of a Lancaster bomber shot down by Günter Grass's anti-aircraft battery during the *Kriegsjahren*; the crew had baled out long ago or been eaten by the little fishes. We settled in.

Towards the end of September the message arrived.

In the wooden postbox by the gate of No. 51 a postcard lay face up with my younger brother's distinctive calligraphy: 'Father died yesterday. 29.9.69. C.'

At the corner self-service I bought a bottle of Jameson and accepted heavy Deutschmarks and pfennigs in change for paper money from mildewed fingernails. *'Danke, mein Herr . . . vielen Dank.'*

'Yesterday' in Killiney was already three days gone past in Berlin, gone already into Time onward rushing at vertiginous speed, carrying us along.

Today in Dublin my father, grown mysteriously young again, the handsome suitor for the hand of Lilian Boyd, rejoins my mother, even younger than he, in beatific bliss for all eternity in Deans Grange Cemetery. In the great metropolis of the dead among whom was numbered Brian O'Nolan alias Flann O'Brien held in high esteem and affection by my fussy mother, all three lying there until Resurrection Day, made one in God.

I walked through Jochen Klepper Weg, broke off some flowering branches of linden and carried an armful into the mansion now lit up like a ship. I put the flowering shrub into a vase, measured out two generous libations of ten-year-old

Jameson and sat in the sun-room to offer a silent toast to my
departed gentle progenitor: 'Upriver always, Da!' That which
we are must cease to be, in order that we may come to pass
once more in the body of another. Padre, be still, and exist
anew! (A page was turned, an old man sighed, leaves fell from
the linden tree. Tracery of leaves, tracery of leaves.)

Upstairs it was uproarious bathing time. My sons were
having hysterics, all three of them like seals in a Germanically
large and accommodating bath, with the windows thrown
open on the incessant birdsong in the garden and surrounding
woods, the air inside permeated with the scents of bath salts
and unguents and Pear's soap and flowers. Your glass of wine
stood on the edge of the handbasin. You were soaping them
and washing their hair and sang 'Frère Jacques, Bruder Hans'
in an inspired Esperanto mixture of German, Spanish, French
and English, and they were laughing their little heads off. To
learn is to submit to having something done to one.

What I would hope to convey, reader, is movements from
the past (movements of the hidden heart), clear as sand in
running water; the strange phosphorous of a lost life nameless
under the old misappellations.

There are days when we scarcely know ourselves; days
when we do not properly belong to ourselves; assailed by the
strangest of feelings and moods that are perhaps forebodings
of our last end (in the form of stupendous sundowns), with
cattle bawling in descant, and the Connemara hills of
Gorumna and Lettermore (formerly small islands) reflected
inverted, standing on their heads, in tarns gone lapus lazuli as
the sun goes down, as if gallons of Quink had been spilled into
them, and upended swans feeding at the bottom, at this going
down of the sun again, and the Friesians bawling to be milked
and two seals hunting salmon under the bridge on a strong
incoming tide. What clarity of the firmament blazing and
dancing above the pier at Bealadangan! The small Starres do
reel in the Skie.

Mysteries: revealed truths which we cannot comprehend.
You can see it any day you like in the streets of Dublin.

Incredulous recognition of long-lost friends on all sides. Some of it of a theatricality which must be suspect, the fervent grasping of the hand while loudly expressing disbelief in the lost one's corporeal presence, while pumping the hand up and down. "Is it yourself that's in it, avic? It can't be! I DON'T BELIEVE IT!!' Manus, Finbar, Paddy, Ronan, Damien, Rory, Danny, where *were* ye? A-roaming in the gloaming? These strange encounters are so common that they must be regarded as a feature of the place; characteristic of a small capital regularly depopulated by centuries of emigration, in an expiring light.

On 16 June of 1978, the year I am recalling, the voice of the Hound Dog Man was howling over the city, where I found myself drinking hot rum in Agnew's of Anglesea Street near the quays, a pub popular with bus drivers and conductors. A conductor toting his leather satchel and clipping apparatus stood before me with eyes half closed, holding on to my arm, and his scummy lips sang 'It's a dr*eeem*, oney a dr*eeemmmm*' and he humming like a radiator.

'Whossa greatest singer inna worrld?'

'Alfred Deller.'

'Izzyonnacharrts?'

'No.'

It was Bloomsday and my eldest son's eighteenth birthday, the thirty-third anniversary of the destruction of Hiroshima. It was a lovely blue morning in 1945 when the cylindrical bomb with its packed canister of unholy death came drifting down out of the sky on its little parachute like a child's toy, to explode over a city fragile as if made of papier mâché and some 200,000 Japanese civilians with a great cry gave up the ghost.

13

Los Alamos

Robert Oppenheimer weeps.

Grounded American airmen are ordered to kneel to have their hair and their prayers cut short by one fierce practised swing of a razor-sharp ceremonial sword; the head falls to the earth as the neck opens to spurt arterial blood some distance and a terrible cry hangs frozen on the dying lips and the lungs have stopped functioning. Drenched troops begin 'shogging' (edging) to their right across a hill in Scotland. They had taken up their positions in the wet corn-stooks and tried to sleep, trying to keep their powder dry; Major Hodgson rides along a mucky lane, lost in thought, not knowing that the Protector had decided, after some prayers, to attack at sun-up, send in his shock troops, the Dragoons, show no mercy to prisoners. He (Hodgson) hears a cornet crying in the night, crying for his mammy, for he knows that his hour has come. It is the night before the Battle of Dunbar. Major Hodgson fiddles with his tobacco pouch, coughs, his mount limps, having over-reached in a gallop out of trouble. He does not like the feeling that is growing on him. Someone is watching; someone is waiting; know your enemies.

The harvest moon (tee-tum, tee-tum) wades deep among the clouds of sleet and hail (Carlyle).

The nuclear physicist is sobbing his heart out. He has had mushrooms for breakfast and quarrelled with Bohr. He too has a sense that something very bad is about to happen, but Oppenheimer will not let Bohr know what his feelings are; Bohr is an idiot.

The Pentagon had already authorised the priming of the second knock-out bomb. The next city scheduled to get it in the neck is Nagasaki: they will make a clean sweep of wiping out hundreds of thousands of innocent civilians whose only offence was to be born Japanese and call Nagasaki home. It would be home no longer when the second annihilation bomb came drifting down out of the clear sky.

In the heart of the elemental chaos let loose a dead sun shone fiercely but briefly (candle flame extinguished in mine filled with methane fumes), stronger than the true sun of midday, the Life Giver.

But this was the Life Taker (Oppenheimer had wept) and before the tarry incendiary rain had begun to fall, the double atomic thunderclap had echoed hollowly off Heaven's doors.

But the Americans had already begun to prime their second bomb. The ground war had been conducted without mercy on either side, with grenades and flamethrowers to choke the fox-holes in islands and jungle from Guam to Guadalcanal – names that seemed sticky with soldiers' blood, the dead, the wounded, the dismembered, and those set on fire.

The enemy, Nips or Japs despised and feared, were seen as subhuman, against whom every barbarity and atrocity was permissible; vengeance would be wreaked in full measure by the stronger, deaf to all entreaty.

The logic of total war demanded the infliction of intolerable pain, the more atrocious the better; and in this sense the two bombs were perfect, the fruit of the Manhattan Project that had caused Robert Oppenheimer to weep. They were named as if after beloved domestic pets, Little Boy and Fat Man, and the first B-29 bomber was named after somebody's mom, Enola Gay, homely as blueberry pie.

The Fat Man was in fact Churchill whose V-sign was the fuck-you finger insult denoting cuckoldry; as the rival swastika was the crux desecrated, a torture wheel whereon victims were broken.

At Los Alamos in the desert of New Mexico the Americans, Nils Bohr and the other clowns, made the Trinity Test at 4 a.m. Far away in a filling station a woman saw the sun rise, and half an hour later it rose again, the proper sun rising at the proper hour. The theoretical physicists were screwing their wives like monkeys, carnally committed by nerves and anxiety.

'Why are we all having babies out here?'

In Hiroshima and Nagasaki it would be better for the women *not* to have babies, not just yet.

The fellow who ascended the tower to plant the Trinity Test atomic bomb, closely observed by the wives (already pregnant) of the Manhattan Project specialists Bohr and Oppenheimer, heard ring in his ears the triumphant Waltz and Serenade by Tchaikovsky played over the Tannoy. The Los Alamos valley was thirty miles wide, green on the near side, with orange rocks moulded by sun and water. One observer had noticed a yellow halo about the mushroom cloud which he likened to the haloes about the heads of holy martyrs in paintings by Grünewald; when he might as well have compared it to greenish gangrescent pus on cotton wool covering a war wound.

If the Axis had discovered fission before the Allies, then God help us all. Hitler had his own musical fancies and selected what seemed to him appropriate fanfares to precede Reich network announcements of striking victories in the field as Czechoslovakia, Austria, Poland, France, The Netherlands and parts of Scandinavia fell. The invasion of Soviet Russia, code-named Barbarossa, would be 'child's play in a sandbox,' he told Keitel: he had chosen Liszt's *Les Preludes*, found by Funk and a splendid example of Reichian *Poshlust* matching the splendour of Goering's uniforms, Speer's architecture and Party bombast in general, to be the Nazi victory fanfare or war dance.

Hitler himself had dreamed up the Stuka's diving screech to terrorise the bombed ones below. When he appointed himself supreme commander in the field, *Oberkommando der Wehrmacht*, designed his battle pennant, he saw only what he wished to see (war was all maps, spread out on a thirteen-foot table, a huge block of marble cut in one piece; a matter of straightening out bends, throwing in fresh divisions; the names of places, Maikop, Sochi, Sukhumi merely distractions), heard only what he wished to hear, and kept his soft manicured hands clean in choice chamois gloves. He had thought up a grenade-throwing machine constructed along the principles of the lawn-sprinkler, but its functional purpose was suspect, for it flung grenades back into its own lines, not that this would much inhibit its inspired inventor.

Orders came from on high; he was not prepared to give up ground, the bends in the front must be held at all costs; the enemy position must be overrun. The enemy must be out-flanked, out-tanked, out-gunned, out-produced on the home front (munitions in the hands of Speer), out-manpowered (Schacht), out-ballbearinged. Raus! Raus!

'At all costs!' It should have been stitched in scarlet into his white silken battle pennant with its swaggering dangerous swastika. Face us at your peril!

Now, at the corner of Harry Street and Grafton Street where once the grand old picture house and restaurant stood (Nice Teas a Speciality), I wasn't thinking of Harry Truman hiding behind the long drapes in the Oval Room. This President would have dropped forty atomic bombs on the holy city of Kyoto but had to make do with two, one for Hiroshima, one for Nagasaki.

'Forty years on dis earth,' declared the bus conductor with a desperate sincerity, positively foaming at the mouth, 'an' e'll be remembered frevver!'

Now the flower-sellers were offering bunches of *semper-vivens*, sometimes called immortelles, the little flowers of the Andes, outside the Dublin Savings Bank. The Sign of the Zodiac stood opposite, now in new hands.

In the old days the draymen from the famous brewery at St

James's Gate came there to tether their heavy dray-horses to the railings and let them chomp away at clumps of hay with their big herbivorous buck teeth, pissing like waterfalls on the pavement.

In clumped the weary draymen in their clayey boots, calling for foaming pints. They stood at the bar counter and gazed up with proper reverence at the stained-glass windows above, where the heraldic beasts stomped and ramped in their spotless stalls.

PART III:

Ballymona Lodge, 1985

14

Aboard the SS *St Columba*

One murky morning in mid-January I entered an icebound Euston station in a London under snow. The Holyhead boat-train was running late but the *St Columba* was waiting in Wales.

I travelled there with a young couple not on speaking terms. When they got on the train at Crewe they were already reduced to sign language. She offered him sandwiches, a thermos, fruit; he would accept nothing from her hand but stared out the window with pursed lips. He didn't know her. Having waited until she was finished and tidily repacked, he helped himself. They ate separately, methodically chewing and swallowing, looking out the window into Wales, pretending that the other was not there. They were having a tiff. Presently we reached Holyhead and there was the SS *St Columba* moored to the quayside.

As a heavy hose discharges dirty water, Muzak was being pumped indiscriminately into every nook and cranny of the broad ferry, soaking into each corner of the renovated lounge, into the toilets and into the luridly lit Cardiff Arms Park bar which was doing a roaring trade as soon as the security cage was unlocked; as into the Lansdowne Road bar where a wild-eyed Kerryman paced to and fro like a caged beast.

It must be said that the Irish *en masse* in transit in close overheated quarters are not an attractive sight; shabby as

itinerants, their children already running wild as mice, miscegenation upon miscegenation.

To ram the message home a patriot's hand had daubed in
black paint shiny as tar the divisive equation IRA + INLA =
FF? How damnably unnerving to be among one's own at last!

Soggy sandwiches purporting to be ham and cheese were
on display behind glass guarded by young slovens in soiled
overalls. On the boat deck the baggage master inclined an ear
to the whisperings of an overexcited woman that caused his
cod's eyes to bulge. The silent pair who had got on at Crewe
were *still* not speaking but as black out as before, trailing about
on their own with mulish obstinacy as we moved through a
darkening sea, apparently proceeding in the wrong direction,
into the Channel and open ocean; a sensation familiar to train
passengers in foreign lands where trains enter a station only to
retreat the way they have come.

My *compañero* Paddy Collins the fractious painter and man-
about-town and his late companionable octogenarian friend
Arthur Power, assuredly no sailors, had once for a dare sailed
over the Irish Sea to Wales from Dun Laoghaire harbour in
Arthur's twenty-two-foot yacht that had previously sailed no
further than the Kish or Howth Head. With slop-pail on
masthead as primitive radar equipment they had sailed for
Holyhead, a problematical landfall. Coxman Collins was
alarmed by what they encountered.

Vast ocean-going liners honking mournfully proceeded
through the Channel on set radar courses, sending out wakes
strong as tidal waves. The small yacht grew smaller and
bobbed about like a cork on the swell, Arthur green to the
gills retiring below for forty winks. Every conceivable shape
of vessel moved through the Channel day and night.

They could have been sunk at any moment; they were
nothing on the radar screens. Arthur slept on and did not
appear on deck until Wales was sighted, a headland and Welsh
cattle in a morning mist: Holy Island. Collins moored the
yacht, threw himself down on the beach and was out like a
light. Then they had to face the tricky return voyage.

They made it somehow and sailed into Dun Laoghaire harbour with dewy shrouds in the early hours with all the spires rising up into a pearly Irish sky and the dogs barking a welcome home. A solitary Chevrolet was parked by the pier and binoculars were trained on the intrepid mariners. 'One man at least didn't want to see us back.' Who was it but the cuckolded husband smoking his way through packets of cigarettes, running the window up and down. The buggers were back. As they glided in and made fast to the moorings the big car glided away.

St Columba docked in darkness. A taxi took me to Breffni Mansions through a light fall of snow. I had not phoned and did not know what welcome to expect, or whether the Master was at home. I rang the bell. After some delay (for Paddy now was old as Arthur then) he came downstairs and opened the door, invited me in. I toted two heavy bags.

'I'm staying a month.'

'You are?'

In the event I only stayed the night; we were to fall out before the eventful evening was over. I found two Marquis de Riscal in the Off Licence.

'Shoot the corks off,' Collins said.

In his irascible old age much annoyed him; I had forgotten just how much he needed to be the centre of attention. Patricia came into the house, returning from a bar where she said she had been insulted. I spent an uncomfortable night in a spare bed in the room where he worked amid the smell of turps and oil paint, listening to the lamentations of the gulls. He had been insulting in Normandy and now worse nearer home, the home I was looking for, wherever that might be.

Patricia was up early brewing coffee.

'You shouldn't have to take this from him, Rory, you his oldest friend.'

'I won't any more.'

I took a taxi to Merrion Square to lay claim to my new inheritance, the first *Cnuas*, Charlie Haughey's government grant for needy artists. I found the Arts Council people in

carpet slippers with their feet up on radiators. The paymaster
was in his office upstairs; the first cheque could be issued
immediately.

From there in the ice and slush I took another taxi to the
Trustee Savings Bank in Grafton Street opposite the flower-
sellers and the *sempervivens* and opened an account; then a
third short taxi ride took me a place I knew in Harcourt
Street, a small hotel run by country people, with old wooden
floors squeaky as the Musée Rodin. I booked myself in and
was assigned the same top room I had been in before, No. 23
under the roof. Margaret from Offaly, the maid of all work
whose chores never ended, showed me to my room. My posh
accent baffled her; she probably took me for a Frog.

'What nationality are ye?' she asked, turning the key.

'Irish, the same as yourself. I've been out of the country for
years.'

'And now you're back?'

'I am.'

'It must be grand to be back.'

'Certainly.'

Bad weather followed me about like a faithful hound. In my
long absence the plain Dublin girls had become plainer but to
compensate for that the pretty ones had become even prettier.
They moved delicate and cautious as cats on the icy pavements with scarves about their mouths like yashmaks, joky
Boy George headgear and stripy leg-warmers.

Bay Leaf French-style restaurant had become an Irish-style
antique shop. There was a proposal for all-female graveyards.
Shelagh Richards had died in her sleep, aged eighty-one.
O'Casey had fancied her as a young girl. At the Arts Club
W. B. Yeats asked: 'Who's that girl with the head like a lion?'

'The buses still running?' says I to the taximan.

'Just about,' says he to me.

'Still snowing?' says I to him.

'Annywan with half a fukken brain wouldn't drive today.

Fukken ice – *hard!*' says he.
    'Are we in for it?' says I.
    'I'd say we were,' says he.

A couple of years later my irascible old friend took his leave
of the waters and the wild when widow Patricia and daughter
Penelope scattered his ashes from the banks of the Garavogue.
A young piper played a lament, Anthony Cronin read some
of his verse, a swan took off, the risen breeze blew ashes back
and I may have swallowed some grey particles of thigh-bone
or cranium, taken like communion wafers, as nourishment on
the way.

    Prior to that the widow twice over had looked into the
coffin of her first ex-husband and been taken aback by his tiny
size; neat in a bow-tie he had strangely shrunk. John Ryan
had shrunk in his casket, became an effigy, a totem. Is that the
fate of all dead husbands, in the widow's mind – to be per-
ceived as effigy?

Country people creep about this hotel where the floorboards
creak and the children of the owners run free and shy as foxes,
freezing when you encounter them. In the dark airless bar the
serious imbibers thoughtfully swallow dark pints of stout
pulled by sullen barmen. No television (a mercy) but piped
Muzak all day until the bar closes and then some more until
the last toper collapses. The dulling pressure of circumstances
presses down.

    The pay-phone, full of coins, was torn from the wall by
vandals, Tom the barman tells me. The other phone is in the
office. This is the Hotel of Creaking Floors, what can I do for
you? A female guest complains of no hot water in the bath, no
curtains in the bathroom, no bumf for the loo. I am reading,
appropriately enough, Werner Herzog's diary of a walk he
took from Munich to Paris in the depths of winter to save the
life of Lotte Eisner. 'Sorrow was gnawing in my chest.'*

---

* *Of Walking on Ice (Vom Gehen im Eis).*

My room overlooks the rear of old disused premises once the home of Edwards and MacLiammóir, both now dead, whom I remember well. The house too looks dead, its windows rotting away. The snow has gone; now it rains, a purposeful drizzle. All is dripping and falling away. I have phoned my brother, will look around Wicklow town for winter quarters; having decided against Wexford.

'Don't hit that man!' cried one of the lads armed with snowballs as I came a cropper outside Blazes, the two feet suddenly gone from under me on the icy pavement.

EEC Eurobarometer reveals that the Irish are a little less gloomy about the future than a year ago, while the majority remain pessimistic all the same. Forty-five per cent believe the world situation will disimprove this year. They are not as down-hearted as the Belgians, of whom only 12 per cent believe that matters will improve, while 51 per cent believe the contrary.

Given optimum choice, purely hypothetical of course, optimists outnumbered pessimists in West Germany, Italy, Denmark and Greece; whereas the spiritual suffering of the Swedes knows no bounds and must be unmatched in any other north European country: their social services the best and their suicide rate the worst (the Russians beyond the Urals are beyond the bounds, the Finns remain enigmas). By the first third of the coming century all Sweden will be controlled by a few companies and life become a sort of Swedish Ford plant, which may account for the present high suicide rate.

Women are slightly more constipated than men and the young in the 15–25 age bracket more so than those older than them. Eighteen per cent of the Irish fear world war, as do 25 per cent of the Dutch. The former Boomtown Rat Bob Geldof is again fundraising for the starving Ethiopians, he himself made rich through his philanthropic activities (Band-Aid).

Sufficient to say it's time and weather like this that bind us together as a nation, make us what we are, lackadaisical day-dreamers hardly able to put on our own socks. They say of days like these, with a sweetly dying inflexion, 'Isn't that a *miserable* day?' almost with affection. As if such days were not a constantly recurring misery here in Ireland, among the time checks, weather forecasts, jingles and advertisements.

A *very* cold north to north-west airflow covers all Ireland. Sharp early frost, sunny spells, scattered showers of hail, sleet and snow, some possibly heavy and prolonged but dying out during the evening. Frost becoming widespread, sharp and severe. Moderate to fresh and gusty north-west winds, strong in some exposed areas at first. Maximum temperatures 2 to 5 Celsius. Further outlook: Very cold. Severe frost. Isolated wintry showers dying out. Rain or sleet extending from the south-west.

Sunny spells!

'Fukken ice – *hard*!'

Morning train to Wicklow (it's the train for Wexford). Check out of here. Pack.

15

The Return

Wearing a dead man's castoffs and with his Spanish hunting-bag slung over my shoulder — gifts from Annmarie Suchman a widow of Santa Cruz — I hauled my baggage down to Reception, checked out of the Hotel of Creaking Floors, phoned up a taxi to take me to Westland Row station, now Pearse Street station, named for the patriot and martyr, to catch the morning train that would deposit me at Wicklow station, if it was still operating, where my brother (not seen in ten years) would surely be there to meet me, if all went well. But you never know.

I was looking out for winter quarters, a quiet place to work in, now that I had a stake; but such was my present dreadful anxiety that I was still considering Wexford. Was there no room for me in the world? It was the year after Richard Brautigan had shot himself in the Montana woods. He and his buddies, a gang of moonmad Midnight Cowboys high on angel dust, had gotten too darned fond of shooting out the bunkhouse lanterns.

Grove Press my American publisher also published Brautigan and I had taken to his hip fiction in Spain. My old amigo Deck had phoned my office in Austin from Santa Cruz in southern California across God knows how many time zones to tell me that he was dead, had blown himself away.

I spent Christmas 1984 with the Decks whom I had last

seen twenty-one years before; after I was through the fall
semester at the University of Texas at Austin where I had
been hired to teach Creative Writing, don't make me laugh,
an occupation or pastime recondite as falconry.

After Santa Cruz I spent a week in London with my three
sons and one estranged wife, before crossing to Dublin on the
St Columba in the depths of winter, a bitter winter it was that
year, that murky day in mid-January.

Dublin was icy, the whole city frozen up; walking on the
hard-edged slush was perilous.

I was the only passenger to get off at Wicklow station. It was
not the same station I had passed through thirty-seven years
before when on vacation with Conal Cullinane. By a low
bridge the train had crossed a shallow weedy river and by
rights should have drawn up at a seaside station, but the sea
was nowhere in sight; we were in the country. The portly
stationmaster in uniform was disappearing into his cubbyhole
and the switchman (it was hairy O'Hills) had left his signal-
box to light a fag and stare down at me, then a signal dipped
and the train already out of sight tooted its horn on the way
to Rosslare.

I stood on the edge of the platform with all my worldly
goods at my feet, the 'lifer' released for one day from the
penitentiary in the grand old Russian movie *The Ghost That
Never Returns*.

The signals had changed, the switchman went in and some
linesmen in Day-Glo came shambling along the track, smiting
the sleepers.

'Is this Wicklow?' I called down.

'You're bang on there, boss.'

'It doesn't *look* like Wicklow.'

'Well it's been here a long time.'

'It must be Wicklow.'

I took my bags in both hands and walked out of the station.
There were a few cars parked by the kerbside but I did not see
my brother's, nor did I know what make of car he drove,

something modest certainly. Then, close to, a car window was rolled down and my brother's face looked up at me, grimacing.

'Hello there. Get in. Shove your bags in the back.'

I got in, stowed my baggage.

'I shouldn't be here,' my brother said, letting in the clutch.

Stay, Time, a while thy flying!

'How's that?'

'I'm late for a meeting already.'

He drove in a jerky fashion down the hill a few hundred yards, turning left into a car park among low-lying offices. He said I could wait there; he would not be long. I said that I preferred to wait in a pub. He said he would drive me to the Grand Hotel but I wouldn't like it.

'Why not?'

'An awful place.'

So he drove me there. There was a long curving bar and a big fireplace with a great log fire burning in it and chatty curates pulling pints for a few late lunchers.

'I'll be grand here,' I said.

'I won't be out much before four.'

'That's all right,' I said.

16

Santa Cruz

In Santa Cruz (the Holy City of Oz) on Monterey Bay in northern California the acolytes of High Tech speak in intense and compromising vagaries. Terms once used for 'mind-expanding' drugs are now applied to computers: expand your mind through software, get wired to God! Get with it, man!

A haven for hippies for more than a decade, mall rats panhandle in downtown Pacific Garden Mall, while in the surrounding redwood forests dropouts, drifters, renegades and tree-people live in abandoned cabins and almost literally 'hang out' in tree-houses.

Digital data with mind-bending capabilities is yours to play about with, and the information purports to be the key to the whole new world, a mystical universe where magic comes alive.

Dr Timothy Leary begat Geneen Haugen who begat Allan Lundell who begat Howard Pearlmutter who begat Steward Brand who begat John Lilly who begat Robert Dilts, a Santa Cruz software engineer working on a series of seminars on computer engineering.

In the drug era, people realised it was possible to reproduce the brain, but it was too hard to control. With a personal computer you can reprogram your own brain and you can be in control, it was thought. If you want a message from the

high-technologists, it's the exact equivalent of what the
ecologists are saying. If you look at ecology and you look at
computers, the same rules obtain, the same messages emerge.
We're in a direct feedback loop here. Right? Neat.

We're in a loop in history, man. The world is being
recreated and we're right in the middle of it. People have a lot
of power right now. Right? That's why it's important for us
to spread the possibilities on the higher side of force. Trippy
spiritualism. Right?

Some people are computer freaks from the age of seven.
Some are happy to stay that way. When in doubt, man, punt.

All that stupendous coastline aquiver in the luminous air
has a very Spanish look to it, first appropriated and stamped
there when Father Juniparo the Franciscan monk walked
there, saw what he saw and liked it. He was the right-hand
man to Caspar de Portola, Governor of Baja, California.

Robert Louis Stevenson lived there for four months in
1879, a century after the Spanish development had started,
and found a world of absolutely mannerless Americans,
whereas the Spaniards and Mexicans were doing all things
with grace and decorum.

In the darkness the wind-chimes sound on the balcony and
the seals are barking in the bay and around the wharf.
Anastasia's voice became plaintive, repeating my name over
and over. I cooked you two eggs sunny side up, you drank
three cups of coffee and left by taxi in the dark, near to tears
again. You were flying back to Austin, Texas; I to Copenhagen via Dublin.

A sound like a car horn stuck or a factory buzzer going is
the sound of an early goods-train pulling out of Santa Cruz.
It's 7 a.m. I am lost in the land of illusion, formerly Brautigan
country.

The airport van which took me from Santa Cruz to San
Francisco was driven by an ex-Marine. I was the only passenger and we got into conversation. He told me he had
married twice, had two daughters; one studied English, the
other, law. The first has no knowledge of the world: 'iniquity

is outside her range'.

He served on a heavy cruiser in the Korean war. 'You gotta study your enemy. Unless you know your enemy you're dead.' His recommended reading: Philip Wylie's *Generation of Vipers*.

17

Dream-Houses

My brother Colum, the Dote of Yore, had worked under the architect Lubetkin in London in the Tecton offices. When I arrived he and his wife had been living fourteen years in Co. Wicklow, renting a place at Three Mile Water and working as site architect for the modern village Cooney was building for his wife. Now he was head of the Planning Department of the Wicklow County Council and was building his own house on some land he had bought in Dunganstown East. Patiently as the laying down of petroleum deposits or the snail that moves about with its house on its back, my brother was building his dream-house on a hill.

He had qualified as an architect, as had Max Frisch, Aldo Buzzi and Saul Sternberg before him. He was a person of great patience who showed a marked preference for well-made things, a bit of old craftsmanship, nothing gimcrack for my brother, whose character had been formed early.

Mumu had knitted him a mealy-coloured jersey in fawns and browns like the markings on a thrush and this he wore until it fell off. He dressed himself with the slow solemnity of a priest vesting; it was all ritual, the order in which he dressed – the knitted socks, the boots, the underpants, and so on, and last came the jersey, slipped over his head with a struggle to get the arms free of stitching that had unravelled; this with the priestly pride of the kissing of the alb before he slips it about his neck. Daily for years and years I had watched my brother dressing, standing by the bed opposite mine in the nursery. He had a special intense look of concentration. He preferred that mealy jersey with its yellow specks to all others; it was like the *Mickey Mouse Annual*, a Christmas book shaped like a squat box that we asked for every Christmas, having worn out the previous copy by intensive reading.

That early determination of character (sometimes known as 'thickness' or obstinacy by Mumu) had manifested itself when the Dote took out a subscription for the *Wide World* magazine from money he had saved up, doing chores about the house, running messages, patiently accumulating enough pocket money, not spending it on Rolos.

When he began collecting stamps he bought a stamp album and tweezers, consulted Dublin philatelists, shaking his savings box, a small red pillar box with a slit for the pennies. He probably preferred saving to spending.

When he had read systematically through a whole shelf of the novels of Dickens, he turned to the two shelves of Scott's Waverley novels.

My brother was thorough in all he did. Hereabouts none called him by his Christian name; he was Mr O'Hills to the Beltons and the Cullens and to Jim Phelan, the father of nine. Dim-witted Hughes had brought him a blinded jackdaw to look after, intuiting a hidden compassionate nature; the lamed and broken had an appeal.

On my first day he came three times to the Grand Hotel: once to deposit me with my bags, then to say the meeting would delay him, until at half-past five he condescended to take a drink – a half of Guinness. He invited me to sup with them.

The nameless low-lying abode was on Dunganstown hill just off the narrow by-road, guarded by earthen embankments, so that you would pass and not see it from the road, for no chimney stacks were visible, no windows revealed any interior, no name (Ard na Greine was popular all over

Ireland) graced the gatepost. But it was in there all the same, crouched down and hidden by its earthworks and plantings of saplings – a cross between a Russian dacha in the woods and Robinson Crusoe's ambuscade built into a hillside, not intended to be seen.

It had the functional look of Crusoe's makeshift compound, thrown together with material that came to hand; part stockade, part granary, a homestead not drawing attention to itself, like its owner.

All this I would discover on subsequent visits; on the first night I saw only the interior, and that was strange enough.

There was a touch of the rough rustic about it. The *russkaya izba* of Russian log house made of great logs of dark wood that could rot in time; one thought of snow falling and serfs crouched over dying fires. Here was a shabby variant of Marxist André Lurçat's '*maison minimum*', the house-of-few-things, a simplified plebeian dwelling-place.

I thought again of the prototype, of the marooned one, Crusoe and how he had put together a dwelling place ram-shackle yet strong from the parts of two disintegrating ship-wrecks; of the Tule tree-house 2,000 years old in Mexico, a functional abode that could contain whole communities of simple folk who dwelt there like birds and bees in Cowper's 'boundless contiguity of shade'.

This functional austerity, an austerity so much a factor in my brother's character and reasoning (use what you have), brought to mind the house that Wittgenstein, a true lover of the austere and unadorned, had designed for his sister; said to be nothing more than supporting walls and beams. The alcoholic Flann O'Brien, homeless in his own home, dreamed up slaphappy subterranean dwellings. Giacometti had a dusty grey studio filled with narrow forms and piles of old news-papers.

I remembered the great yew tree in Springfield garden, the oldest there, spreading its shade over the tennis court, a feeding place for missel thrushes and blackbirds all summer long.

Up in it my brother and I had constructed a tree-house – a raft (actually a stable door) in the sky, hauled up by ropes and warped about thick branches; on to which we took our provisions, cats, Daisy air-rifles, reading matter (*Hotspur* and *Beano, Dandy*); and if we stayed still nobody need know we were there.

We could have stayed there for ever.

Elizabeth Bowen has written: 'I had heard of poverty-rotted houses that might at any moment crumble over one's head; but this one seemed to belong to those edifices more likely to collapse not through decay or inherent faults of construction but because, alas, all building materials are perishable as our own bodies and like them fated to fall to dust. The walls seemed thin as rattan and the roof joints groaned as if they could already foresee their end.'

The purity of their seclusion was unimpaired by either telephone or television and as my brother wrote few letters and his wife I suspect none at all, their seclusion was total, kuskykorked up tight. And since they had no telephone I came unannounced, greatly to the dismay of Stella Veronica, for visitors were few and far between. The Mini was angled in under the lean-to and my brother advanced to break the glad tidings. I brought two bottles of Marquis de Riscal, not having seen them in ten years.

'We have a visitor.'

In the shocked silence that followed there came an appalled whisper:

'Who?'

'Rory.'

She gave herself up for lost, vanishing, vaporised into thin air, pleading a sudden headache; at least she was not in the narrow galley kitchen nor in the living room. Perhaps she had fled upstairs, both hands clutching her temples? My brother found a corkscrew with some considerable trouble and I opened one bottle with practised ease, to let it breathe.

The Russian cats – fabled creatures oft mentioned – were strays found on building sites and befriended by my kind-hearted brother, taken home and permitted every freedom of the house, sleeping on their double bed and walking across their table, 'laws unto themselves' as my brother put it.

My brother and I dined off our laps by a dying fire like characters in a Gogol novel, served silently by the unseen wife who remained invisible throughout the frugal meal but for the white nun's hands that passed condiments through the serving-hatch.

We sat by each other in the ingle of a fireplace cramped enough to be thought Tudor, the low chimney-breast decorated with small tiles painted by the owner, seemingly at a time when chimneys had just been invented.

An arras of careful drape of cotton batting made for a snug retreat close to the fire. The chimney opening was low to the ground and drew badly, sending out puffs of smoke from the flue. A few briquettes smouldered in the grate. It was a constricted hearthside, the easy chairs were uncomfortably low and we crouched about the fire that was slowly expiring, while the Russian cats flitted about upstairs in the privacy of the gallery and glared down at me through the banisters.

'This is a really nice wine,' a precise white voice enunciated from the galley.

Presently stewed apples and custard would be served out with Swiss roll and tea.

'When will it be finished?' I enquired.

'Nowhere near yet,' my brother said. 'To say it is half finished would surely be an exaggeration.'

'Well, dream-houses never get finished. Look at Gaudi's La Sagrada Familia in Barcelona – God's *casa* still roofless in the Ramblas.'

After supper, wedge of Swiss roll in hand, my brother offered to show me over the premises. I was first taken into the kitchen, narrow as a trawler's galley, from which the hostess had fled, perhaps up the uncarpeted wooden stairs, and was even now hiding under the bed, uttering silent screams.

But no. The bedroom was confined as a Union Castle

cabin; one could barely stand upright in the centre of the narrow way. The inset dormer windows were just beyond reach, pitched at an awkward angle into the sharply sloped roof.

It became stifling hot in summer, stuffy and impossible to ventilate in winter. The half-tame rats ran races above their heads and pissed on to the bed, my brother told me. He would have to do something about it sooner or later; perhaps knock out an opening to let in some fresh air, but of course that would admit the cold too.

Great feculent piles of old newspapers, magazines, periodicals and folders bulged from a shelf low down, while more of it showed under the bed. The high cabin was partially masked by a hessian runner. We went downstairs again and I was shown the bathroom. An old-style bathtub squatted on stout little legs on a wooden dais, the bath itself piled high with old grey washing that looked as if it had been seeping there for days or maybe weeks.

'The wash,' my brother breathed into my ear, as if admitting to something shameful.

Dostoevsky had defined eternity, Tsarist Russian style, as a bathroom full of spiders. But where was Stell?

I was in for a surprise.

My brother pushed open an unpainted door without lock or bolt to secure it that gave into a carpenter's rough shed open to the elements, with apertures for windows not yet in place, smelling of putty and cement, with a single unshaded 40-watt bulb that lit the grey figure who sat bowed down on a kitchen chair set into the bare earth. She was gazing raptly at the soil at her feet, hands folded in timeless resignation on her lap, as if beholding the very foundations, the roots, the worms, the teeming decay. The pose was pure Whistler's Mother but painted by Sickert.

'Oh hello Rory! Long time no see,' said Stella Veronica, unsmilingly, still staring at the earth.

My brother quietly closed the door on this eerie apparition. It shook me, taking me back to the time when we were poor in Greystones. My brother had written from London, asking me to call on Shell and 'cheer her up'. She came to the door of the parental home in Greystones harbour, a rubberised 'hotty' clasped to her stomach, invited me into the chilly parlour, the closed-up room where none but guests were taken, and played 78 r.p.m. records. I told her to put on bonnet and shawl and took her to Lewis's Hotel just up the way where I bought her a Gordon's and tonic with my last half-crown, served by Patsy the barman who was reputed to wear a corset.

With a wristy twist betokening long familiarity I now uncorked the second bottle of Rioja while my host attended the dying fire and we sat warming ourselves about it, recalling old times in Celbridge and Greystones. Until gradually, slow as the incoming tide into Greystones harbour, whilst still remaining out of sight but throwing appropriate remarks from various quarters, now from the gallery above (as if dressing herself, preparing to go out), now from the atrium (as if admiring her husband's watercolours of Greystones and Bray Head, all framed by himself), now near the front door (as if about to take her leave), now (very muffled) from the bathroom (oh horrors!), now (plucking up courage, getting ready to make an appearance) saying something witty through the serving-hatch with a silvery laugh quickly cut short – until at last Stella Veronica shyly parted the arras and joined us about the fire, accepting a refill.

They showed me their drawings in pencil, each compulsively drawing the other's face, the loved face, or their own, as if drawing distant hills, always the Sugar Loaf big and small, Bray Head and Greystones harbour, generally in winter when the front was deserted. And Stella Veronica's oil paintings and papier mâché busts of heads done twenty years previously; for all these were mementoes. And they repeated the names over and over, familiar as the beloved landscape, Val Hinds and 'Bunch' Moran.

My brother told me that when the cowboys had departed and when their botched work had been corrected, he found himself hammer in hand on the roof at midnight, knocking nails into the slates; until one of the Russian cats that had climbed up the ladder after him put its paw on the nail-head and stared into his face, intimating that it was time to down tools, call it a day.

'It showed more sense than you,' I said.

The closed-in life they led seemed to suit them; they did not need friends any more than they needed telephone or television, giving all their love and affection to the waifs and strays that came their way (the cats, the blind jackdaw, the badger that ate its way through a wall), and the pets kept dying off, until the overgrown garden had become a veritable pets' cemetery.

The room I sat in, all the rooms of the house, looked as if they had never been swept or cleaned. They had one of those old-fashioned hand-manipulated carpet-sweepers that house-wives used before electricity and Hoovers came; but some-how one could not see Stella Veronica in headband and apron getting into every corner, washing and dusting, setting the place to rights. It was like a child's tree-house, and dusty naturalness a part of its charm. The scale too seemed off kilter, better suited to a couple of dwarfs in a fairy tale. If she was too timid to ride a bike (oh the brakes!) Stella Veronica could hardly be expected to clean a house; and her husband, who didn't notice, really didn't care. In such a peculiar functional dwelling as this one, notions of clean and dirty hardly applied.

Cordially invited to spend the night (but where? between them, pissed on by the rats?), I declined, saying that I would try the Grand Hotel whose off-season rates were reasonable. When we had finished all the wine and the Swiss roll and said all we had to say my brother drove me back at breakneck speed along the narrow twisty roads. The headlights failed twice, but he drove on at unabated speed. He had bought the Mini second-hand for £1,000 and she had never given him any trouble, touch wood, yet.

'Why bother about style if reality is already two-thirds illusion?'

Brother Colum had always carried common sense to absurd lengths: that was the way he was made, the way he thought. To the slapdash and the meretricious he opposed an inflexible will. In a letter he had written of 'interminable hours of building work with which I have been engaged for the past seven years and will be for some unknowable years to come.'

Together with Stella Veronica he had cycled into Soviet Russia, to Leningrad to see the collection of early Impressionists.

On sagging telegraph wires suspended on crude poles swallows the size of partridges went *weeedy-weedyweed!* just as at Springfield in the 1930s when we were children.

18

Cycle of the Hours

The lyrical Gallic gloom of Marcel Carné's *Les Enfants du Paradis* and *Hotel du Nord* were very much to brother Colum's taste.

On the grey penitential stones of Greystones harbour my brother and Stella Veronica undressed on either side of a rowing boat winched up above high tide, discreet as the sheet drawn across the room in Capra's movie *It Happened One Night*; the sheet separating Clark Gable from Claudette Colbert.

Stella Veronica ('Shell') was the youngest and prettiest of five pretty daughters, namely: Derithea, Conchessa, Fanchea, Gilliosa and Stella – and brother Gilmar (who rarely ventured out of doors) there to protect their honour. As soon as they arrived in London they married strong bony men with bank balances and jobs in the City and bachelor apartments around Wimpole Street.

The emaciated cyclist and architectural student Colum O'Hills pursued her wordlessly at first, throwing lingering looks before accelerating off as though borne on fragile diaphanous wings to supper in Kinlen Road on the fringes of the Burnaby.

Shell, still single, had the sticky eye of a pollen-glutted bumble bee that can neither sting nor stay nor fly away, fixed with longing for my brother, the ace cyclist.

He, burning midnight oil and applying himself to his studies, travelled to and fro by train, from Greystones to Westland Row and thereafter on foot to Earlsfort Terrace. The evening brought him back again to the bicycle shed and Willie Doyle and Kinlen Road. After supper he brought out his papers and studied by night.

One morning, foodless, he fainted in the urinals of the university. Coming to he found himself alone and on the flat of his back, with seagulls squalling and fleecy clouds passing overhead; he did up his flies, got to his feet, left the urinal.

His hands turned faint blue and then duck-egg green after diving off the harbour wall at low tide, a tortured corkscrew that attempted to copy the famous diver Eddie Heron, followed by long immersion in the cold sea. A knightly display of valour put on for his ladylove who watched breathlessly from behind drawn curtains in the Mulvihill home abutting on the harbour. Then (by this time they were talking) she was handing him his threadbare towel on the harbour wall smelling of fish. She was soon to be seen on his crossbar, my brother inhaling the meadowsweet and columbine of her flaxen hair, in his seventh heaven, flying past the Eden Hotel or parking outside the Ormonde Cinema.

The starved anxious whippet face was that of Pierre Batchef the hero of *Un Chien Andalou*; Stella Veronica was Dita Parlo, the child-bride and waif on the barge in Vigo's *L'Atalante*.

In the days before they were married – when he had qualified and moved to London to work under Lubetkin – the cyclist faithful unto death phoned long-distance and when he was connected burnt her initials (S.V.M.) on his wrist with his lighted cigarette, as he heard her dear distant voice through his exquisite pain, come all the way to London, as knight of yore encountering his beloved swooningly attempting to press past him on narrow turret stairs presses burning lips to her inside arm, that intimate place, causing her almost to faint, her eyes closed; he begging a boon, to know what trial or tribulation he should undergo to earn her love.

The terms of the marriage contract were not binding enough for Stella Veronica: *till death do us part* did not go far enough; she wanted them to include eternity too, which she hoped to spend with her grey-faced young husband. My brother stubs out his lighted cigarette on his wrist as the dear voice whispers sweet nothings for his ear alone, all the way from Lewis's Hotel (S.V.O'H), my brother sobs.

His attic in Buckland Crescent, Swiss Cottage, had a stink hard to describe – coal-slack and perdition, rank as a dog kennel. In those Dostoevskian living quarters under the rafters my brother worked as one condemned to it. And there began his conquest of the great grimy city immense in extent with its millions of inhabitants, that spread itself about him in all directions.

Head clearance was adequate if you happened to be no taller than five feet eight inches. Certainly it had a strange odour all its own, a stink of poor man's clothes mixed with stale cooking smells, a dire musty pong that belongs to unremitting poverty – at one time it had probably been the maid's room.

Smells were long trapped there. He lived on oatmeal porridge, Heinz beans, cheese, rhubarb and Bird's custard, bread and milk, the beginning of his vegetarian regime. Which was more or less my own diet in far-off Ealing Common, in a room rented from a French couple who feared that the end of the world was nigh.

I sometimes called to borrow small sums of money, and pound notes were produced from the battered cardboard suitcase he kept under his camp-bed. He cooked his morning porridge on a single gas jet; heating was supplied from a single-bar electric fire.

To ventilate the attic and liberate some of the more offensive stinks long trapped in it he raised the skylight a few notches to admit the muggy heat of August or the freezing foggy air of December that penetrated into the lungs like poison gas in No Man's Land.

In a London heat wave he lifted his work-chair on to the

zinc table and stuck his head out the skylight and worked there undisturbed even by the constant drill of traffic. He was his own overseer, with his pencils and reference books and T-square, his own cook, banker, manservant, tutor, librarian and supervisor, his own man. And he loved Stella Veronica Mulvihill most dearly and intended to make her his wife.

And so he did.

'Why is my blood turning blue, Colum?'

Stella Veronica's finger joints are wrapped in dirty rags like little mummies and secured with Cellophane which binds these rags too tightly.

'Shell doesn't believe in breathing.'

19

In the Hall of the Mountain King

Stella Veronica's moody brother Gilmar was an indoors man. He said that everybody spent their life indoors, except perhaps the tourists who walked about the streets. I never spoke directly to Gilmar, for his distant manner did not invite such approaches. I heard him in another room playing 'In the Hall of the Mountain King' on the hand-cranked gramophone.

When it stopped Stella Veronica asked 'Are you listening, Gilmar?' speaking in the same low conversational tone she was using with me, to find out whether he was listening at the door.

Do the habitually silent ones endure a constant tumult and commotion, a disturbance of the suppressed emotions akin to the disturbance of tinnitus, a Bay of Biscay nausea? Sarah O'Donnell, toothless as an old woman, who had lived all her life on Inishere, used to complain of constant noises in her head. Day and night she had the din of tinnitus in her inner ear.

The mother crept about the house, quiet as a mouse, venturing out for provisions. She rolled an orange under her bed before she got into it, to find out whether a burglar was hiding there; she would surely know if the orange didn't come out the other side. All the mad Mulvihills were like that, creeping about, a bit cracked.

Gilmar seemed to be fascinated by the O'Hills, the four brothers living on the edge of the Burnaby in a cottage only intended for summer use.

'They never go out. They spend their time looking at themselves in mirrors,' he told Stella.

When the Mulvihill daughters refused to feed him any more he took to dossing down in the deserted rugby club (now Hickey Field) where my brother fed him scraps from the O'Hills' meagre larder.

We, the grand O'Hills of the swanky Burnaby, were no better off than they, the poor Mulvihills of the harbour. We all moved about on bikes, summer and winter. Stella Veronica herself spent much time indoors.

Sometimes Gilmar, sick and tired of the house and gazing at himself in the mirror and playing 'In the Hall of the Mountain King', would primp himself up and lacquer his tennis shoes for a rare public appearance, posing on the steps as if anticipating applause.

When Gilmar broke out into the open after years indoors in the damp harbour house or living like a dog on scraps in the deserted rugby club it was to take up a very precarious peripatetic life awheel as unlike the sedentary life which he had led before as you could imagine.

He took up with his friend Alan Foster who had walked out of the office of his father's shipping firm in Dublin after one day's work there and had decided there and then never to return.

They went cycling around England together, knife and fork tied with coarse twine to the crossbar, the togs and towel clipped on to the back carrier.

Until Foster met a rich Australian who was looking for a gardener to look after his many lawns. So Foster took the job and went to Perth to mow a rich man's lawns. He wrote back that he was made for life, and asked Gilmar to join him. But Gilmar wouldn't go.

He continued his own cycling about the roads of England, with his bare necessities on the carrier, and many out-of-the-way places from Minehead to Exeter and from Perranporth to Portland Bill saw him, not hairy because he could not grow hair on his face, but wiry and tough like an itinerant, and they heard his songs, a sort of mockery of Irish ballads, the diddley-diddley shit become solemn as he sang 'Come Back Paddy Reilly' or 'Phil the Fluter's Ball'. Until he went too far, or the itinerant life became too much for him, and he was sent into an institution for his own good, to get a change of clothes; a place where he could be fed properly.

His friend Noel Ferns from the haberdashery near the bridge visited him there.

Gilmar asked him, 'What do you think of snow?'

'I hear it falls from the sky in winter, Gilly.'

'No, no, you got it wrong, Fernsy. It comes up out of the ground.'

20

Some Suggestions for Brightening Up the Home

I sat in the back seat of the Mini and smoked roll-ups and Colum sat sideways on in the driver's seat, chomping methodically on soggy cheese sandwiches prepared by Stella Veronica, staring into the damp car park, a tarred area near the sea.

'Why not move into one of the many B&Bs dotted about the town?' my brother suggested, pulling an extraordinary face.

We had considered a mobile home propped up on bricks, in the lee of a dripping pinewood near Three Mile Water, looking over the valley. It was actually a Dublin tram cut in half, hauled there by tractor. We had looked at it; it was a good deal less grand than the railway carriage at Rethondes on the edge of the forest of Compiègne.

We stared out at the deserted car park and the grey sea over which grey wintry clouds moved.

'I knew a man once who lived on a canal barge moored in the Surrey docks. As the Thames rises and sinks twenty feet twice a day on the tide, it was like living in a lift,' I said.

Colum took up his bottle of milk and swallowed some of it, rolling back his eyes the way hens do.

The canal barge *Humbaja* was long and narrow and constructed of unusual material (aluminium) by two Italian brothers who had previously concentrated on manufacturing ice-cream. In summer the condensation produced an inch or two of water in the galley; it was an object of terror in the Camden dock when it came off its moorings. In it my former free-living friend traversed the weedy waterways of England, passing through hundreds of locks *en route* to Humberside.

In his cups and strapped for money he bartered *Humbaja* for a smaller vessel; and that for a smaller one again, until he sold out for a push-bike and then it was shanks's mare and the towpath.

'Chekhov once slept in a second-class railway carriage abandoned on a disused track,' I said.

My brother still chomped on his sandwiches and looked out on the unappealing view, the low sea, the empty car park, a tar barrel that served as a skip, wheeling gulls.

'The view from the Infirmary,' he said.

On the stroke of 6.30 a.m. in came Mick the yardman smelling powerfully of anthracite and abattoir in boiler suit and hobnail boots to give the fire a poke and refill the coal scuttle, and another Infirmary day began in bed at CWC with gossip and regular meals and dozing with glamour puss 'Dog's Hole' Maguire, 'Titch' Fennelly and Donal Crosbie in adjoining beds.

Outside the rain fell in sheets. We had beaten Blackrock in the semi-final of the Senior Rugby Cup at Donnybrook and the sadistic Prefect of Studies 'Boozy' Barrett fell dead of a heart attack.

21

My First Arrival

My first arrival into Ireland was my entry into life proper, head-first between my mother's chubby legs in a Dublin nursing home. My first view of nature was at Springfield in the big front bedroom with a view of distant hills, the cows in Mangan's field and Killadoon Wood.

A day or so later, 4 or 5 March, I was bundled into swaddling clothes and woollen cap and bootees, clasped in my mother's loving arms in the leathery-smelling back seat of the Overland proceeding at a stately pace out of the city, through Lucan and left before the Spa Hotel on a narrow by-road to Naas.

At Springfield my two elder brothers impatiently awaited the late arriver, five years after brother B, seven after brother D. Another two years elapsed before the squalling of brother C would complete the quartet.

Soon the four of us were living in uneasy proximity, until brothers B and D were packed off to boarding school, first Killashee Prep School with a French order of nuns, and then Clongowes Wood College with the Jesuit fathers.

Brothers A, B, C and D were conceived and born in the order: D (the silent, the fingernail trimmer), B second (the buck-toothed), myself third, giddy me; then sound C bringing up the rear.

The four of us were to convene at Springfield; old Mrs Henry from the back road was taught to cook some rudimentary dishes by my mother; there was Lizzy Bolger as maid of all work and Gina Green was called in from the village for emergencies (unexpected guests from down the country). Nurse O'Reilly was there to look after my mother 'when her nerves went against her'.

We lived in a Georgian mansion in increasing rural dilapidation as the years rolled by and with them my father's fortunes, as property and real estate in Los Angeles were sold off and no more fat cheques came rolling in.

Between us and the brown River Liffey reared up the high boundary walls topped with bottle glass that marked off Killadoon estate owned by descendants of the infamous Lord Leitrim; a grand Protestant estate into which Catholics were unwelcome except as day labourers on push-bikes or moving manure by wheelbarrow.

22

Wicklow Town

Wicklow town is situated at the mouth of the River Leitrim at the foot of Ballyguile Hill some twenty-two miles south of Dublin. Vessels can enter the harbour at any state of wind or tide. Ships of 2,500 tons can discharge cargo. In 1641 General Sir Charles Coote had his soldiers set fire to the church where the townspeople had taken sanctuary on what is now Melancholy Lane. On Gallow's Lane public hangings took place of the 1798 rebels, including Billy Byrne.

The great cable-layer Halpin was born there. He retired there, having laid some 25,000 miles of cable, and died in his home at Rathnew. The little town was granted a Royal Charter by James I in 1613.

On the second Sunday after I took up residence I walked out on the back road past the Columban Missionary Convent and the new golf course and the bungalows my brother built for Cooney, his boss, a three-mile walk to Wicklow town. Robins were singing in the low hedges and a little girl was feeding hot gruel to a pup at a gateway.

'Am I going right for Wicklow?'

'Straight down. You'll see a big town in front of you. That's it.'

I went down. And there it was.

Cords of wood on the quayside were waiting to be shipped

off. The Leitrim Bar was by the river.

Penetrating into Cooney's wood, a young fir wood very piny underfoot, I couldn't find the path leading up to the knoll and came out again, causing a lemony guard dog to bark and keep on barking as I passed by.

Distant figures, larger than life, were walking about in a purposeful way on the new golf 'track', toting buggies behind them, past bunkers, far away. The winter greens were spiked and sanded, the air blew cold from off the sea.

I had my photocopying done at Flitterman's drapery and shoe shop. They were closing, unable to get insurance against burglary, after five break-ins in the past year. The criminal fraternity was prospering.

Meanwhile up in Dublin, in the Horseshoe Bar of the Shelbourne Hotel on Stephen's Green, in amiable juxta-position sat Randal, Count MacDonald of the Glens, the Honourable Garech de Brun, heir to Guinness millions, and Lord Henry Mountcharles whose forebears had stood shoulder to shoulder with or near enough to William of Orange, King Billy at the Battle of the Boyne, the upshot of which upsets and disturbs the body politic to this very day. The young Lord Mountcharles lives in some considerable splendour at his ancestral seat at Slane Castle, the grounds of which are let out for rock concerts.

In Wicklow I stayed three days and nights in the Grand Hotel and then signed an agreement to share a modern bungalow with a single lady, one Dervorgilla Doran of a ripe 44 years, who had converted a rundown County Council cottage with outdoor toilet into a comfortable home in the Japanese style, Ballymona Lodge. I rented it for a year. I was assured that the owner would be away most of the time. There I would find the quietness that Julien Sorel knew in prison. There I would become quieter than humus.

I would also be required to feed and exercise a large black Labrador, the guard-dog Blackie. Solved, for the time being, 'the torment of no abode'.

Tommy Cullen has suggested that I buy the cottage abutting on the cemetery near Three Mile Water.

'It's owned – oddly enough – by a Protestant lady, a Mrs Hall. She is being driven mad by her relatives and would let it go for £2,000.

'I'd have the Hughes family as next-door neighbours,' I said. 'They're mad already.'

'You could sell it in two years and make a profit of £2,000. That's not bad.'

'Homeless' must be one of the saddest words in the language: the condition of houselessness. Pity the homeless. Some bright suggestions from well-wishers for my new abode:

(a)   a B&B in Wicklow town
(b)   a Dublin tram cut in half;
(c)   a rundown cottage by a cemetery.

Bizarre.

Melancholy Lane is named for the massacre of Wicklow townspeople, men, women, children, grannies and dogs burned alive in the church by order of Sir Charles Coote. The 'mere Irifh' need expect no quarter; no sanctuary for them in their own church; a wailing throng were driven in like sheep to the slaughter, the door barricaded up and the place ignited.

Coote had no more compunction about getting rid of them than if they had been a nest of rats to be pitchforked. The screaming congregation in that fire are very remote from us and refuse to be focused in the mind's eye; themselves as carbonised by Time as the fifty-four luckless French prisoners asphyxiated in Kinsale in January 1757.

I could no more imagine them in their last agony or as blackened heaps in a gutted church now being rained upon, open to the elements, than I could imagine Davies the tramp in his heyday driving the first Baby Ford ever seen in Wicklow down the main street to the consternation of dogs and townsfolk. It must have caused as much rumpus as did

Faulkner's dashing Major de Spain in his new red EFM with cut-out blaring, passing and re-passing the Mallisons' house in Jefferson, Mississippi.

St Patrick himself thought twice about landing on Irish soil after his coxswain or steersman or whatever he was, one Manntain, had all his front teeth knocked out by stone-throwing and catcalling natives who ran along the shore, wild as troglodytes brandishing sticks and defying them to land. Now he has a church named after him there. The mate, was he?

The Murrough or 'plain by the sea', where I set off one day walking the fifteen miles to Greystones; the Black Castle, Paidin's Rock, the three lighthouses, one functioning, are all sweet landfalls in the Land of Nod.

23

Interrogatory

Here's the author and co-tenant and the bane of his life, Dervorgilla Doran, at parley. 'I always thought it would be right for a writer,' she said.

'You've got one now but is it the right writer?' I said.

'I might even begin to write here myself,' she said.

'Oh I shouldn't do that, Dervorgilla.'

'Why not?' said she.

'It's not you,' said I.

'No?'

'No.'

'You'll look after the house for me?' said she.

'As though it were my own.'

'Don't get too fond of that idea.'

Her three sisters, all raging beauties, were, in order of appearance

Parma Pipina Assumpta,
Caterina Perpetua Emeraldina
Dolota Bobolina Ubeda

(for mother Doran pregnant with her third daughter had been reading the great Russian masters). Dervorgilla was the fourth and last-born daughter.

Mrs Agatha Doran was a stern matriarch.

Thirty thousand condoms have been imported into the country since 1980. The anti-condom lobby fears that 'soon the floodgates will open'. Fourteen thousand Irish emigrated to Britain during the 1940s and 1950s. The official figure in 1985 was down to 6,000; today it would be more like 30,000.

A weak winter sun all day with smoke drifting over Clinton Binnions's field. The school bus passes the gate at four, a package of toys arrives for Dervorgilla from Japan, addressed to 'Ballymona Edge'.

Dervorgilla and Rory co-habiting were as separate and apart as it was possible to be within a small area, the feminist lady being very insistent upon 'one's own space' *pneus* flew back and forth, as with Frederick the Great and Voltaire in Sans Souci. 'Shall we go over the books tomorrow?' began and ended with Rory writing out a large cheque, always double what was anticipated, rent being frequently asked for and paid in advance, for Dervorgilla protested she was 'strapped for money'; meek Rory never questioned her strict accountancy. The bungalow was shipshape as a yacht, pristine from stem to stern. Dervorgilla left me a note:

'Air-locked taps in a disconnected water-supply can do damage. Advisable to keep a small supply of fresh water as reserve.

When the water is cut off, be careful not to draw too much in bathroom as pipes may air-lock (or burst?).

Should this occur, the air-lock is easily removed. Use hose (from patio), connect other end to air-locked tap. Switch on both taps when water supply is renewed, to force water up into air-locked pipe.'

Dervorgilla with her flaxen hair cut short and her quietly assertive manner, leans on her friends as on a feminist sorority, and puts me in mind of those formidable early feminists who would brook no obstacle. Women of the stamp of Lady Hester Stanhope, the young Baroness Blixen (wasted by venereal disease but still managing a coffee plantation in the

Kenya highlands, shooting lions), Freya Stark the octogenarian traveller and linguist learning Persian in her extreme old age, Mary Kingsley travelling alone in West Africa.

'Where is your husband?' they asked Mary Kingsley.

Her clever reply was calculated to disarm.

'I am searching for him.'

Bluestocking and suffragette with something of the later briskness of the kennel-maid slopping out at 6 a.m. are mixed with positively militant qualities, or better still, the sterner piratical backbone of the pirate queen Granuaile who sailed to London and spoke with the Virgin Queen as an equal, in Latin; these her innate qualities.

'My Lord, you know what you were before I made you what you are now. Do my bidding or by God I will unfrock you,' Elizabeth had addressed one of her froward archbishops; that was pure Dervorgilla. If she was determined to have her way, she got it. But in my brother she had met her match. He was beholden to nobody, was immune to coercion and threats, refused to take bribes, was endowed with the patience of a galley slave.

Planning permission was required for the mobile home brazenly parked in the paddock, and planning permission Dervorgilla would not get. They both dug their heels in. The mobile home was a fixture in the paddock with Dervorgilla's friends coming in and out. Every time he saw it my brother ground his teeth.

'Would you mind telling her that that thing is illegally parked there and will have to be moved?'

'And who will move it? The County Council won't annoy her even if it's contributing illegal rents and contravening God knows how many laws.'

Dervorgilla began a vendetta against my brother. She conducted it rather as the Boer farmers waged guerrilla warfare against the British Army by stealth, knowledge of the terrain and superior cunning.

'Your brother's an impossible person to deal with. Did you

know he is greatly disliked around here? Why is he doing this to me?'

It was a striking feminine ploy. Dervorgilla wanted my brother's guts for garters. She had met her match: a will obstinate as her own. My brother must have been the confirmation of her worst fears, being even cagier than herself.

24

The Bum Bailiff

Polyphiloprogenitive Joe Fallon the needy, breedy father of seventeen, or was it nineteen? I was never sure, any more than Joe himself, prematurely aged by breeding, honorary bum bailiff and permanently disgruntled odd-jobman about the place, has been summoned by phone from Bavaria to give a final trim to the lawn. He performs this service with the utmost ill-grace; I see the set face under the battered hat going to and fro behind the spluttering mower chewing up stones.

The dispossessed one never meets your eye, nor does Matty Doran: Biddy's quiet man cannot rid himself of the stink of pig slurry, of servitude, working a ten-hour day at harvesting. He works for Herbst the German.

Mylie works for the German too and is another one who will not meet your eye. Perhaps direct eye contact implies social equality, might even constitute a challenge, a threat. 'Take that bold look off your face,' my father used to say, giving me a poke in the back; 'get back into the house, you little brat.'

With those three it's not so much subservience or shyness or cringing before social superiors, but more a matter of reserve, of manners, slyness, country cuteness. Joe Fallon can never set foot in the old homestead again, unless invited in; the council cottage has been transformed beyond recognition into a modern bungalow, no more the old shabby place with outside toilet constantly occupied. There he had brought up almost two score children, fed them, set them up in life.

The nearest he gets to it is the kitchen porch, Blackie's quarters; he must never presume to pat the Labrador on the head any more than he would presume to shake Dervorgilla by the hand. Blackie would have gone for him, as the loyal animal goes for the unhappy postman darting from his van; as he would go for all such intruders.

Jim Phelan, father of nine, salutes me from the mobile home roof and addresses me as 'Sir', which makes me feel uncomfortable. 'The Finisher' is Dervorgilla's nickname for Phelan. It was Phelan she called in to finish the job when she had exhausted herself working on the drains and walls, injuring her back again with the jack-hammer; until she had worn out all her helpers and the boyfriend had fled back to Australia.

Joe Fallon the erstwhile owner and she the grand single lady, a speaker of foreign languages, secure and sedate in herself and her possessions, her cushions, are poles apart socially and could belong to different races. The man who once owned the cottage and the acre and a half of land, now works there part time as her handyman. The man who once owned the property outright now trims her hedges, cuts her lawn and scythes her paddock, rakes the gravel and humbly accepts mugs of tea and biscuits from her hand, and acts as a sort of unpaid overseer or bum bailiff when she is off in foreign parts.

Many an acrimonious aside did he make to me, addressing my ear, to the effect that he had been badly diddled in the transaction and made a fool of; the day after he sold for £6,000 he could have got £17,000 in the open market, as was known to the party that purchased, her smart Dublin lawyer and the tricky estate agent. They all knew that and laughed behind his back. He had been badly taken in.

It could of course be said that he himself had never recognised what he had or the possibilities of the place; the grand view over Binnions's long field and the rolling hills beyond. For Joe the run-down cottage and the bit of land that went with it was all that he might reasonably expect in the way of worldly bounty, his due here on this earth. And all it represented was so many chores, his wife endlessly big with another child, the endless feeding, the endless upkeep of property already falling to bits.

A field was a field for all time and nothing more than that and he need not expect anything grander. Whereas Dervorgilla had to travel to Japan to see what could be done at Ballymona and at no great outlay (£2,000 down payment secured the property). She, so often strapped for money, saw what could be done and she did it; transforming the place by stripping the walls back to the brick, digging drains, installing a bathroom and modern kitchen, knocking out windows to get a better view.

What would the likes of Joe do with a view? Views were beyond anyone with so many children to rear.

When Dervorgilla had let out Ballymona Lodge to other sub-tenants, Ned Ward had acted as her bum bailiff, arranged the letting and collected the rent. When Dervorgilla returned he handed over £1,000 in cash. A commission had been mentioned and a few hints had been dropped, bum bailiff now feeling very foolish; but nothing came of this and Ned did not care to press the point. He received not a penny for his trouble. He swore that he would never do it for her again. 'Dervorgilla watches the pennies.'

Biddy Doran (no relation) the cleaning-woman comes twice a week with her two brats. She tells me that the Wicklow people are an unfriendly lot, unlike the Wexford people; wasn't she herself born and reared there and intended to return? She ran a stationery shop in Gorey, 'before Lara came along', as she coyly put it. Then along came Laurence with the snotty nose, the image of his da and 'stands just like his granda'. Biddy had big ambitions for him and probably saw him as a doctor or lawyer. She wanted to get him out of the fields.

Matty's existence is all drudgery or near enough to it, labouring from six in the morning until nine at night for the German, overtime paying his taxes. While the well-off Herbsts are off skiing in Switzerland with governess and the two kids, Matty is bringing in the Herbst harvest and Biddy feeding their cats and dogs.

25

Fumes

A pall of rank Virginia tobacco smoke hangs in the
Periwinkle Bar, enfolding all in its mysterious embrace, dense as a gas attack by the Boche on the
Western Front. The Periwinkle is a bar of some decrepitude
patronised by the disorderly youth of Wicklow town. On the
morning I slunk in it was deserted but for an English visitor
downing an imperial pint of lager and his small daughter
hanging on to the pinball machine that was firing off coloured
lights. Some friends arrived and began to talk in their strange
fractured English.

'Yew git outah bed inna mawnen an luke aught d'windah
an ooow d'yasee?' (Pregnant pause, rolls eye, gulps lager.)
'Nuffen. Nabaddy!' No work, see. He's got into the routine
now and stays in bed until 11 a.m. Early rising is not on
(Hockney would not have approved of this slackness). 'It ain't
flash, see. Wot's the point?' The will to work has gone.

There's a power of grim dark pubs in Wicklow town. But
grim and dark as they are they are not as grim and dark as
those of Carraroe in remotest Connemara beyond Gorumna
or Newbliss on the Monaghan border which was too grim
even for the bold Dermot Healy and thus must be adjudged
the pits.

I myself go to the Leitrim Bar by the river, a pleasant stroll
past the Garda barracks and over the low bridge. Arc of a

rainbow above the harbour where a long freighter from
Bilbao is offloading a cargo of slag, waiting to take on logs,
packed into a great pyramid on the quayside.

The Leitrim Bar is usually deserted when I arrive in the
morning or around midday with my provisions in plastic bags,
for a few drinks before I phone Sadie for the taxi back.

See here.

A pool table, vapid radio music to make you dizzy, a TV
screen in the public bar for the horses, a view of the stormy
sea outside the door, with a rostrum for live music in the
lounge to be avoided at all costs. Dowling himself serves me
a half-Guinness and Jameson chaser, way-out 'ham' sandwiches smothered in mustard, here's health.

Da Dowling is the father of eight in this breedy corner of
our fair land: four redheaded sons will carry on his name and
no doubt the Dowling breeding propensities. He spent the
morning rolling empty iron lungs into the yard; he is his own
cellarman, after being a butcher for most of his working life
in Birmingham. Three years ago he entered the bar business
and hasn't he got it made?

Clear sky again after three consecutive overcast days. Walked
into Wicklow by the back road, past a yard with two savage
Alsatians that attempt to tear down the gate to get at me.
Snow on nearer hills. Called on Dervorgilla's cleaning-
woman Biddy in Herbst's gate-lodge. Toys and tricycle
strewn about the entrance. Large TV screen adding its heat to
already overheated living room, the young Roddy McDowell
in racing silks. Two brats nagging each other and tormenting
the cats that glide in and out. The Quiet Man takes his grub
in the kitchen. The German Herbsts are about to depart for a
skiing holiday in Switzerland. Biddy will feed their cats and
dogs.

Am advised by Butler the chemist not to buy expensive
eye-drops, Optrex will do the trick. As he is making out the
prescription he gives me a penetrating look. 'Don't I know
you?'

I retire to Healy's Bar for some peace and quiet. Am I or am I not the same person I have always taken myself to be? And in that case who am I? It is better to be precise than to be imprecise; for you can be imprecise in many ways but only precise in one way, the correct and only way, or so a Chilean nuclear physicist once told me in Texas. Only in such discipline can we hope to find freedom, if it exists. How many facts does a life story require? What is fact and what life story? No, it is not enough to live; you need to know as well.

The butcher with bloodied hand and forearms, as if he had just beheaded Mary Queen of Scots, recognised me stepping fastidiously into the sawdust and called out 'You're the pork-fillet man!'

Woke this morning to hear my name called, and raising the slats of the venetian blind what did I see outside but my brother's greenish visage under the rim of his porkpie hat pressed to the streaming glass. He was *en route* to the office and had stopped by on a business call, and yes thank you he would accept a Nescafé. Why not? He wore a soiled muffler and wool gloves as his only concession to winter and the perishing cold that he as a vegetarian must have felt acutely; as acutely, I thought boiling the water, as he felt everything that might touch his solitary vexatious nature.

My brother was not what you might call a sharp dresser. His new hound's-tooth tweed jacket that had been bought off the peg for £40 in a Dublin haberdashery was identical to the one he had discarded, having worn it daily for fifteen years; Identical even to the pen and pencil protruding from the breast pocket, the tools of his trade.

Would I ask neighbour Ward whether the screeching of the power-saw at the farm on the Blainroe crossroads could be heard in his place (Ned's). And if so did it disturb him? Did it constitute a nuisance, in a legal sense? The woman who was objecting lived at the crossroads and claims that she couldn't talk to her friends; she couldn't hear them talk, and was 'almost weeping' – this imparted with a shake of the head and a titter, the stock response which my brother has for all human foibles and the distress that sufferers seems to bring upon themselves.

I said I would ask Ned. I didn't hear it myself, being around the corner and protected by a stand of saplings.

Tuesday, 8 January

Streams of water invade the waterlogged fields. Cycle to Brittas for milk and mulling wine. I see surf breaking on a deserted beach and the tide out as I pedal up the hill under the cawing crows in the tall trees coming into Brittas and passing the dim-wits' summer quarters now closed up. A beardy puck-goat glared at me over the low wall at Three Mile Water where the twisty road ascended towards the little cemetery. The puck-goat is old Hughes himself. My brother's first home was in Cullen Cottage where he had as neighbours the extended Hughes family, some of them with their wits seriously astray; gone crazy as hares from sheer misery, like Faulkner's Bundren family burying the granny.

There were all-year-round dim-wits at Three Mile Water and a summer contingent to be found in the holiday homes outside Brittas, supervised sipping their soft drinks in the dim recesses of McDaniel's in the daytime.

The Hughes family disperse themselves in mobile homes raised up on breeze blocks and are to be seen toting shovels, cutting up wood on the saw-horse, mooching about or gaping over the low wall at passers-by.

In the boggy place a silent mongrel watches me fly by. January proceeding; dark by 4 p.m., bright evening star; lit wood fire at five, night comes down early. At Cullen's shop Una dragged herself out of the *Irish Press* to tell me that yesterday's cortège was for Alec Stone's father who died in his eighties. Tommy attended the funeral; she tended shop.

The storm promised by the weatherman last evening is even now approaching the western coast and will reach the eastern by midnight.

At 1 a.m. it struck with dramatic force and blew all night. Next morning a strange bird with drenched feathers was preening itself on the fence.

My brother says that he doesn't understand Aristotle. Happiness, not goodness, is the end of life. We choose happiness for itself, never with a view to anything further; whereas we choose honour, pleasure, intellect, because we believe that through them we shall be made happy.

Cyril Connolly maintains that this is a restatement of Santayana, who said that happiness is the only sanction in life and where happiness fails 'existence remains a mad and lamentable experiment'.

Connolly added the rider: 'The heart is made to be broken, and after it has been mended, to be broken again.'

26

'Cash' Murphy Appears

It is virtually impossible to move about unobserved in the country, particularly on foot, where your every move is observed and interpreted. Dervorgilla told me to be sure and lower the venetian blinds in the room of my new home when I venture out, for the poachers who pass unseen through Cooney's wood keep a sharp eye on Ballymona Lodge. So I do all that when I walk out or go by bicycle: lower the blinds, double lock. Keep wits alert.

I cannot say 'Stay!' to Blackie the black Labrador who is young and foolish and follows me everywhere, to the beach, to Brittas, to Wicklow, causing an unprecedented uproar at the butcher's and upsetting the local dogs. If I want to go out unescorted I must do it surreptitiously, on the sly, like a thief, creeping silently about the house, watching until Blackie dozes off in the patio and I can slip out, tiptoeing on the grassy verge, not on the gravel, slipping out on to the road and left by Ned Ward's cottage, closed up, past the baying Alsatians until I come to Blainroe crossroads and sharp right by Kilpoole tree nursery, safe now; and down the hill with the first gladsome sight of the sea risen high above the trees, and a stocky fellow leaning on the gateway with his back to me, apparently watching the farm machinery working on the slopes below.

'Hello there,' said he to me in a familiar way.

He is a high-coloured rough man with wild blue eyes, bursting out of his skin but full of cool cheek. Why did I go on the lower road? wasn't the other shorter? why did I do that now? I said that I preferred this way because it was quieter. He asked me what I did.

I wrote radio scripts for the BBC; I was a radio writer, I said. I felt him watching me as I walked away. He knew who I was, the new tenant of Ballymona Lodge, Dervorgilla's guest; he knew that as well as had the two poachers in the nuns' grounds. They all seemed to know. I felt rather a fool, telling him this.

'Fancy that now,' said he.

'Cash Murphy,' said Ned. 'Have nothing to do with him. Cash is as mad as a brush. Lock up when you go out.'

Mad as the mist and snow was Cash Murphy. Lock up your daughters and your spoons. His redheaded brothers were all villains, Biddy told me. Redheaded villains.

One day he jogged by in a rhubarb-red tracksuit; another day he staggered out of a gripe, carrying a large pane of glass, presumably stolen. This mad red burglar would steal Dervorgilla's cushions from the mobile home the night I had the Laits for dinner; Cash would also remove the sparking plugs from the car parked by the front door. Ann Lait was the auctioneer who told me of Ballymona Lodge.

Walking the back road I felt I was less likely to encounter him. If he saw me setting out for Wicklow he knew he had me, with hours in which to empty the bungalow and mobile home, take what he pleased: stealer of cushions and auto parts.

When Dervorgilla (batting her eyelashes like a coy geisha) had explained what she wanted, Cash nodded, gallantly stripped off his shirt, spat on his hands, blessed himself and knocked the creosoted fencing posts into place with powerful blows of a sledgehammer, displaying a goodly ripple of the manly muscle that had so enchanted Dervorgilla; and the undulating fence rose up like a dream.

Dervorgilla had got the idea from the clever Japanese,

designers of miniature rockeries, stroll gardens and the like, who speak of 'borrowing' the garden. You are led by a winding path which, with short side-spurs, carries through the entire garden and back to the starting point. You must take sightlines into consideration, redesign the lie of the land, pulling as it were the valley into the living room, as in a Bonnard canvas the rumpled sheets of a double bed resemble clouds and vice versa, or Turner's interiors resemble tempests.

The fence must be of uniform height but it undulates to match the valley which it confronts and to which it conforms, the slope of the land continuing into the house, seemingly containing not only Binnions's long field and grazing Friesians but Clinton himself, a shadowy figure in the cabin of his careering agricultural machine flinging out feed while manfully struggling with the controls.

Binnions's herd of newly milked and apparently newly washed Friesians stroll majestically on to the sparkling morning field with the aplomb of a cast of stout Restoration ladies powdered and primped in velvet and lace coming fully costumed on to a brightly lit stage, disturbing a flock of feeding crows that scatter above them, announcing more rain on the way.

A 'vigorous depression' is approaching our shores. Hardly a day goes by without another murder being done, and in the most public of places; and vile knee-capping punishments, more often than not the knees of innocents. Polymath Sean V. Golden has left Brixton and is *en route* to China on academic business. He is a friend of Ned Ward's.

'Cash' (so-called because he never has any?) has the gingery colouring of MacMurrough's foot soldiers, gone from the fields into the first line of battle, fearless wild opponents, open-air men who know the traps and indentations of the land as they know their own hovel. He has been barred for life from McDaniel's who rather go in for family parties and discourage drunkenness on the premises.

When his dander was up he had the strength of a hundred

men, John Stamp the barman tells me. 'Cash is highly strung.'
When in a red fury he reverted to type, became battling Con
of the Hundred Battles, became Finn himself. What possible
use would a hero like that have for Dervorgilla's precious
cushions, the covers 'lovingly sewn'?

My Second Arrival

My second entry into Ireland some half-century later also occurred in the depths of winter and was no less upsetting and nerve-racking, except this time I knew what to expect.

Again the uncomfortable journey over water, the darkening way, apprehension about the welcome awaiting me, palpitations in smoke-filled low-ceilinged lounges, Lansdowne Road bar and Cardiff Arms Park bar, and crowded companionways, the groaning bulkheads, the vomit in the scuppers, the children running wild, the wash of waves without, and always the muggy air of the interior of the ship. The SS *St Columba* wallowing through the murk was due to dock at No. 2 Pier, God willing, more power to Him.

My parents had lived out their last years in a squalid basement flat in Haigh Terrace near the Garda Barracks in Dun Laoghaire and my wife and I were separated when I stepped again on to the gangway and the cold winter air struck me in the face with flecks of snow, for it was snowing again. Freezing air gushed up from the harbour below while a skinning wind blew from the north-east with scuds of icy snow falling out of a freezing sky as I stepped on to terra firma.

The Haughty Horsewoman

Brother Colum has had a run-in with a haughty horsewoman. 'Hi there, you!'
So sang out the haughty horsewoman, rising in her stirrups to get a better view of the miscreant grovelling in his miserable potato patch.

'Barked' might be nearer the mark, from the throat of her so massively astride the big grey gelding, pointing with her whip at my brother who a moment before had been bent over the assiduously manured drills but had obligingly straightened up with a meek smile, and every appearance of craven shifti-ness. 'Stop doing that!'

He was a little late in getting down his British Queens but he could swallow his pride and after all what were a few more minutes lost in the vast aeons of Time lost already; and who was this imperious lady ordering him about like a coolie in a paddy-field?

'The weather's been unseasonably warm of late, and to tell the God's truth so am I,' tittered the brother in his lackey's tenor, giving a suggestive hike to his working trousers that adhered to his thin shanks, white skin visible through layers of repair. 'Swimming weather.'

The haughty horsewoman stared down speechlessly at him as if examining a bug or turd. Her wide-flanged nostrils flared and her constricted bosom heaved.

'Don't you dare get bolshy with me, you impertinent upstart! Don't try me too far!'

'Oh no, ma'am, certainly not,' said the brother, reverting
to type and cringing.

The proud rider was darkly flushed and it became her. The
whispery voice had sounded subversive in some creepy
unspecified way that she could not put a finger on; she
suspected that he was mocking her.

'Pah!' she spat out. 'Out of my path, peasant!' and spurred
her great dappled steed onward.

February snow on nearer hills, ice in Blackie's water bowl.
Dublin householder (this from *Irish Times*) shot intruder dead
with shotgun kept under bed. In the old days pisspots were
kept there but mother Ireland has modernised herself won-
derfully, with power-showers and *en suite* shower rooms.

Of the annual 10,000 break-ins and burglaries more than
half involve violence against the person, but it is not advisable
to shoot an intruder, even if he is armed.

Now some sums. It costs the state £22,000 per annum to
keep an Irish person in an Irish prison, where they will
certainly acquire bad habits. If not already TV addicts, as the
heroin habit, they will become addicts in the Joy. Benzedrine
to kick-start the Joy day, Seconal to end it.

Of the half-million dogs on the island, how many worry or
kill lambs and gravid ewes at lambing time? What does that
cost the farmer in dead livestock? What does it cost the dog-
owner? (Many won't buy a dog licence.) I can live on less
than half what it costs to house a person 'doing time'.

The Irish Sea is half a mile off, hidden behind Cooney's
wood. On disturbed nights you can hear it muttering to itself,
tossing and turning in its disturbed sleep. It is a most consoling
sound and lulls me to sleep.

By the open gates of the Columban Missionary grounds I
met a broadshouldered bigbeamed water-eyed farsoonerite
farmer in shitcaked wellingtons who was knuckling the ducts
of his weeping red-rimmed eyes with a rawboned hand.

'Hard day!' said he.

I asked how the lambs could survive in the freezing snow. He told me that they were hardy enough and would survive.

Passing through (trespassing) the Missionary grounds on my way to the Nuns' Beach a month previously I encountered two rough-looking poachers who said they knew who I was and where I was staying, and this, mark you, on only my second day of residence at Ballymona Lodge. The tom-toms had already announced the arrival of Rory of the Hills.

29

Lambing Time

From Blainroe crossroads comes the high whine of a power saw chewing up planks. Beyond it stands the Approved Stud whose yard, ever awash in pig slurry and liquid cattle manure, would turn your stomach.

I prefer to walk the back road by the new golf course, arriving in Wicklow via the Green Hill. Male and female figures attired for golfing march this way and that, pushing or pulling buggies, replacing divots, recovering from shallow bunkers, lining up putts on spiked greens, replacing flags and striding towards the next tee. It looks a purposeless sort of open-air activity that you might not think to associate with pleasure, unless you played the game yourself. As with other pleasurable activities (chess, copulation, fly fishing), it *looks* ludicrous until you give it a try.

At Blainroe crossroads were some cottages crowded together in cosy familial juxtaposition, two of the cottages accommodating the copious overflow of old Fallon's overactive loins, ten stall-fed daughters and seven redheaded sons, milk-stealers and lurkers in hedges. I called one day with an order from distant Dervorgilla; she would like the lawn cut and the hedge trimmed. I was directed to the middle cottage, which throbbed with stereophonic racket. When the door was eventually opened I saw the huge TV set straddle the floor before which flushed daughters and bawling babes sprawled, sucking and chewing at the fast food that never left their hands. Talk about the fury and the mire!

The fields around are in frantic stir at lambing time, placentas blowing about like refuse and the newborn lambs eager at the teats, two of them lifting the patient ewe off her feet. The ewes are worried, seemingly confused by the struggling outline in the sac that is feebly trying to break out into the air. If the ewes by accident find themselves on their backs, they cannot get on their feet again, piteously bleating; and are defenceless against the grey crows for twenty minutes after giving birth. The parturating ewes have no inkling of danger as the predators hop close to pick out the eyes of the newborn lambs.

'Don't forget that the grey crows have to feed their young too. It's our fault for domesticating the sheep,' so says Ned Ward, dog-slayer and authority on country matters.

Wild sheep are a hardier breed better able to fend for themselves, more akin to the wildebeest that breed on the run when harassed by lionesses on the teeming Serengeti plains. *Their* young must start running as soon as their hoofs touch the earth, for the lions have their young to feed too. The Great Butcher has generously provided a larder for all; the grand cycle of creation has slaughter at the centre of it.

Strychnine to kill the grey crows is laid in a freshly killed rabbit, and fixed as bait in the fork of a tree. The mongrel 'Rags' finds it, devours the rabbit and with it the poison, races home howling to die in his own back yard. The wife is frantic, but the husband knows the cure; he takes 'Rags' by the hind legs and whirls the little dog around his head, as though he would throw him a mile. 'Rags' howls loud and long, expecting to have his brains dashed out against the wall; his master, the hammer-hurler, has gone stark mad. The dog vomits up the strychnine in sheer fright and recovers. Strychnine has therapeutic effects, being a tonic and stimulant if taken in moderate doses.

The mistress of 'Rags' herds a little flock of those who are 'wanting', i.e. not quite all in it, not right in the head, up the hill from the holiday home and takes them into McDaniel's, where they get very excited ordering up Deasy lemonade.

30

A Bat at Evening

Nature will return, my brother firmly believes, because we have too much. Too much of what? Why too much of everything, too much surplus, or what we don't need and very likely don't want.

He is joyless, or joyful in a strange way. A bat at evening.

Statistics show that in the west of Ireland one in every four people over the age of sixty is afraid to go to bed, but sits up all night saying the rosary with a loaded shotgun to hand. They are afraid to take sleeping pills lest they be murdered in their sleep. Three or four gangs are operating, robbing farms in remote areas of Roscommon and Mayo; thuggery is rampant in Sligo and Donegal and the young ruffians are slipping over the border. The old people take pep-pills and hardly ever pull off their clothes, afraid to sleep, their nerves shattered.

All who suffer so are neurotics. The importance of politics in one's life can hardly be overrated; but today you cannot buy a loaf of bread without being in some way involved in politics.

American Presidents Truman, Eisenhower, Ford, Kennedy, Nixon , Johnson, Reagan were ever apt to prate of 'our freedom', and the 'free world', meaning capitalist democracies; Reagan visiting his homeland (Ireland) in a bulletproof raincoat like a G-man, Nancy with terrific facelift smiling bravely by his side.

Politicians live in another world. In any case politics concerns itself only with the things that can be talked about; you have to figure the rest out for yourself. The nostrums of X and Y are as incomprehensible to me as Hubble's evidence of an ever-expanding universe, baffling as the quantum theory. *Twice* as baffling.

In *Image* fashion magazine the names of the owners of beautiful homes featured are suppressed for security reasons. Stamp, the young barman at McDaniel's pub in Brittas, refused to give me a figure for weekend's takings, saying he would be an eejit to do so. An attempted robbery by the Dunne gang down from Dublin had been frustrated by the Special Branch. But the takings are stolen the following Monday and a week later Stamp's two-stroke motorbike disappears. He tells me that he and a friend are saving up to open a nightclub.

Laragh Inn near holy St Kevin's church was sacked by the Provos as punishment (revenge) for the drug-dealing that allegedly went on there – a sort of knee-capping of guilty property by this illegal organisation so keen on retribution, tit for tat. The Provos claimed that it was the headquarters of a cartel of known drug-pushers, one of the ringleaders well known to me personally.

Ned Ward makes miniature hurley sticks for the American market. The cartoonist from Disney Studios draws Irish leprechaun cards of elfin awfulness. On the patio of Ballyhara Lodge the Japanese Zen priest took deep breaths, looked out over Clinton Binnions' field; never before had he known such serenity and peace.

Ten peacocks parade about the renovated grounds at Kilpeddar. The former mucky yard has been transformed into a paved courtyard with swimming pool, the plastic porch of the Queen Anne mansion replaced by a granite Queen Anne porch, the belltower good as new, in distinctly German taste. Years of Irish neglect and rot, bad management and eventual bankruptcy have given way to Germanic *Ordnung*. Regard the Regency mirrors, the Boissy and Georgian fireplaces, the stucco plaques by Creedons, the Curragh oatmeal carpets with thick pile, the Anatolian rug as table cover on the heavy glass table made by local blacksmith Harry Page, the pale pink chairs of Italian baroque.

Brother Colum and Gilmar Mulvilhill – once Gilmar overcame his reluctance to venture out – were great ones for taking the air and hiking about and they knew the fields and seasons, the ditches and hedgerows and copses of trees around Greystones and Delgany as well as poachers get to know their particular terrain.

Gilmar had cycled around England and into Devon to sing his maudlin Irish ballads and come-all-ye's in rural pubs until his health broke down and as John Clare before him he found himself in an institution for the insane out of which he was never to emerge. He got to like it in there. His true friend Ferns visited him on Sundays. He knew no other kind of life than the one he knew now and didn't have to worry about himself ever again. Institutional existence with sedation pills and regular meals suited him down to the ground. Nineteenth April, a lovely washed-out blue day as if rinsed; the itinerants' piebald ponies stand out on the headland most surreally. The growth starting despite the chill wintry air and first swallow flies over Magheramore beach. A dead seabird shot on the sand.

On the bridge *en route* to the Leitrim Bar, the tide is coming in and young lads with lines out for crabs are using lumps of pink meat as bait. The crabs pulled from the river crawl about in the grass; the tide continues to come in. A bumble bee with wet wings crawls across the patio, attempting to take off from the lower step; it cannot and crawls in circles as if drunk, stinging the dry clods of earth I had turned the day before.

'Sheshudda knocked it down,' says Joe Fallon, limp father of seventeen, a gloomy bugger if ever there was one. His old council cottage is now the modern bungalow Ballymona Lodge of unthinkable cleanness and ladylike neatness.

He prods up and a new spud with a brown and broken fingernail. 'Rubbish. The soil's no good.' Unable to bring himself to look me in the eye he shuffles off, halts to say 'Summer end', staring at the overcast sky. What can he mean? Clinton Binnions could have objected to Dervorgilla digging her drains so close to the fence; but he never objected. Fallon objects to everything, a true farmer.

Twentieth April, Hitler's birthday; an Arian fascinated by fire.

Elderly men with polyps in their bowels require careful watching, close observation; and President Reagan is one such. This is the latest prognosis of his physician in the White House. The President's bowel movements will require careful watching and must be closely analysed to determine what course of treatment is best.

In Spandau Prison in Berlin two prisoners remain, one of whom will never be freed. Albert Speer, with none else to talk to, talked to his shadow; for Rudolf Hess, the lifer, is off his rocker. He may not even *be* Rudolf Hess. Who then was it crashed the Messerschmitt in Scotland? Who was the *Über-Hess* making the peace-feelers?

Years later he told Speer that the idea of the flight had come to him in a dream of supernatural forces. A fortnight after he had defected, Speer sent flowers to his dying father without however revealing the sender.

Great flocks of crows pass overhead each evening at nightfall, coming from their feeding grounds along the coast, heading for their nesting places in the wooded valley. Always there is one straggler, an ageing crow last to leave the wheatfield after the main body has departed from the communal scoff-patch. As it flies on into the darkness of late April the safety of the communal buzz must seem to recede and recede as the old crow struggles onwards.

Crows live nine times longer than man, says Hesiod.

Outing to see friends in Thomastown in Kilkenny. Saw a stoat with a young rabbit in its jaw near Baron de Breffni's castle. Spoke to a traveller on the platform of Thomastown station who had seen a white owl near Bagenalstown.

Dublin in April rough as Reykjavik, wintry chill in late April, and sooner or later you meet a madman in the street.

After many years' absence and strange adventures (Cyclops, Scylla and Charybdis, Circe's cave, the singing sirens) Ulysses returns home jaded and saddened. He is not recognised; only the dog remembers him (I have forgotten its name); home seems strange to him.

Ulysses himself did not recognise Athena at first.

Robinson Crusoe marooned on an island defends his home, dug out of a hillside, with a wooden stockade of pointed stakes; primes his muskets, sharpens his cutlasses, affecting to be a fortress fully manned, and prepares to sell his life dearly against the man-eaters who paddle in from another island.

From an armchair in the living room I can see a line of hills maybe twenty miles off across the valley. Hundreds, maybe thousands, of crows pass over at dusk. This will be my home for the predictable future.

31

Anastasia and the
Seven Dervorgillas

Dervorgilla, two-faced as those stone heads on Boa Island, gave me her sworn promise that she would be out of the house during Anastasia's ten-day visit from Texas; she would do the decent thing and make herself scarce, stay in the mobile home and only avail herself of the kitchen for meals. She would keep out of the way. But did she? She did not.

When Anastasia arrived there seemed to be about seven Dervorgillas in residence, strolling from room to room and immutably present like Lady Brett Ashley in Hemingway's great novel. Ballymona Lodge was contracting; with one of the Dervorgillas seated in the kitchen brewing up Earl Grey while another strolled in the garden with trug and secateurs; soon to be joined by a third in bikini for sunbathing, with Ambre Solaire, sunglasses and paperback, *The Quiet American* by Graham Greene, a novel full of lies. While a fourth Dervorgilla emerged radiant from the bathroom, after enjoying a good long souse, to be joined by a fifth Dervorgilla face creamed and in dressing gown, phone in hand, all prepared for a long gossip with a friend in Ballinaclash. Two more Dervorgillas occupied the master bedroom, discussing us in low voices. There could be as many as four Dervorgillas gossiping together in one room at one time, and no room for myself and the truly quiet American whose drunken Russian grandfather had broken his neck after a fall from a loft in Tiflis.

We took to walking on Magheramore and Magherabeg with Blackie, walking to bars in Wicklow and coming back by Sadie's taxi with Blackie whining and slobbering.

'This won't do at all,' I said. 'I didn't invite you here to share a house. We'll take a train.'

I questioned Biddy about the car-hire situation in Wexford and was given the name Mylers.

'Absolutely no hassle,' Mylers' man assured me.

I phoned my namesake hairy O'Hills in Wicklow station and was given train times; soon we were seated in Sadie's van *en route* to freedom.

On the third day we would return the mud-caked hired car to Mylers together with keys and road maps. There were some extra expenses and the £60 quoted had become £100; I had paid out a similar amount at Lawlor's Hotel in Dungarvan.

I saw a familiar face at the wheel of a Hillman Minx proceeding at a stately pace along the seafront; what was Seamus Heaney doing in Wexford in mid-week, and did he drive a car? Somehow Seamus did not seem the type; a push-bike and a long Oxford muffler would be more his style.

We walked along the seafront at Wexford and passed a number of low shebeens until we came to a narrow one with the name *J. Banville* emblazoned over the door in flowery grot. SMOKE CAPSTAN said a slogan on a tin plaque with gruff male hail-fellow-well-met straightforwardness. Player's *Please!* piped up the companion scroll in a softly appealing feminine voice, cozening, teasing.

'Shall we try this?' I asked Anastasia.

'OK.'

And in we went. It was a narrow functional sort of a chilly place such as were to be found everywhere in Ireland at one time but now are on the way to becoming extinct. Modest unpretentious places with Formica and ring-board, not exorbitant to imbibe in, if not particularly agreeable in themselves, fagsmokefilled drinking crypts. A rumpled cleanshaven bullocky man in crumpled snuff-coloured two-piece suit that sagged at the wide seat as if it belonged to a bigger man was leaning across the counter, thoughtfully picking his dentures with a spent match and studying the racing columns of the *Irish Press*, a low paper established by Dev and only good for starting fires. He did not appear to have backed any winners today.

Seeing patrons entering he straightened himself up, stuck out his welterweight's underslung jaw in an oblong face as if kneaded in grey putty or knocked out of shape in the ring. Brush-cut hair stood up stiff as hog's setae on the crown of his bullet head.

'What can I do you for you folks?'

He enquired our wants in a low sincere voice, the modulated tones of a sacristan or undertaker's mute; he had not expected customers at this hour. Half-imperial pints of Guinness with Jameson chasers, right you be.

The publican's name was etched or stencilled athwart the fly-blown semi-translucency of the bug-smeared glass

e l l i v n a B . J
rentniV desneciL

Banville (supposing it were he) served us our chill half-pints and shots of Jameson, placing the former carefully on the Guinness mats supplied by St James's Gate and giving the cold counter a perfunctory wipe with a damp rag.

'Are you Banville himself?' I asked civilly. 'By any chance?'

'Well, you could say that I'm *one* of the Banvilles. It's a common enough name hereabouts. Are you looking for him?'

'You wouldn't, by any chance, be any relation to *the* John Banville, the Kepler and Copernicus man?'

'Not that I know. What does he do? Is he an astronomer or what?'

'You could say that.'

He returned to his *Irish Press* and resumed his browsing up
and down the racing columns as the draught Guinness, black
as the Styx, went clammily down into our interiors.

The outer aspect of the port of Wexford – the drenched
seafront, railway sidings, squalling gulls, the huge backsides of
rusty freighters no less alluring and equally uninviting, were
visible through the blurred panes. I called for two more shots
of Jameson.

We did not prolong our brief visit. When waiting for my
change I attempted another bold cast.

'And how are the boys of Wexford who fought with pike
in hand?' I asked jovially. 'Any slight improvement in the
general bowel condition?'

The pugilistic crown of hair positively bristled with
hostility and the lower jaw took on a truculent slant as
Banville shovelled over my small change.

'Gone across to England or joined the Provos,' groaned the
disenchanted publican. 'We have our own internal emigration, you know, like typhus.'

'How's Wexford business generally, then?'

'This town is dead. It died two years back.'

We thanked him and took our leave.

'The wrong Banville,' I told Anastasia. 'Absolute camel.
Our man within is the sort who licks his fingers to turn a
page.'

In the returning train (whose windows as lips that were
sealed, wouldn't open) Anastasia complained of feeling the
cold, her hands were cold, so I said put them in my pocket
(like a warm muff or a hot brick at the Opera), my trouser
pocket, which she obligingly did. And soon, between one
thing and another, she began to warm up, and had to retire to
the Ladies to regain her composure, and returned looking
radiant and sat beside me, and gave a sigh, and I said, 'You're
looking rodent.'

She offered me her small devil finger and said 'Smell that',
which I did and recognised what it was and said 'Lobster

mayonnaise' with relish, just like Blazes Boylan. And Anastasia gave her small tinkling laugh that invoked sleigh bells and reindeers with antlers and a couple eloping in a sleigh piled with bearskin rugs across icy wastes.

And then, as on a *tabula rasa*, came a converging valley of bare brown trees gone purple in the waning light and an estuary with swans upended, arses in the air, as pretty as can be.

On the journey down to Wexford we had shared a carriage with Narbonne rugby supporters over for the match in Lansdowne Road who were travelling in the wrong direction, and had a poor meal at Lawlor's Hotel in Dungarvon and never dined there again, having found the Moorings, where we dined on Saturday, the day of the match. I thought it was only a pub by the water but the owner threw open a door and showed me a lovely restaurant and said 'We're chock-a-block but I'll try and fit you in', and we had a good meal there with good Rioja and Anastasia looked very Russian. We had watched Ireland play France in a very dirty (fouling) drawn game at Lansdowne Road and we lay on the bed and drank Smithwicks and smoked pot and then crossed to the restaurant and it *was* chock-a-block.

And the following night we returned and had a tiff and Anastasia withdrew herself and all future favours in a most frosty Russian manner and walked back to the hotel through snowdrifts eighteen feet high with packs of wolves howling in the nearby woods and was fast asleep when I returned, having stayed up drinking with Alex the owner by the great fire.

She didn't hear my knocking. The cheeky receptionist phoned up. 'We have your husband down here in Reception, Mrs umm Mills and he says he can't get in.' So you opened the door and climbed back into bed, the single bed, and I saw the clasp-knife by the bedside table and we made it up and got back into the double bed and you wept (again) and said you were being silly and you were sorry.

One of those days was my fifty-eighth birthday and we walked about Dungarvan and admired a line of snow-capped

hills and, meeting an old woman who had lived there all her
life, I enquired the name of the hills, but she didn't know the
Drum Hills. Then we drank frothy beer in a pub in Youghal
open to the elements, and then we were on the road again and
you drove like a fury up the backsides of huge lumbering
pantechnicons thundering on and leaving us their wakes of
mud and water and the wipers were going and you pulled out
and pulled out again, overtaking in one of your black Russian
moods that was a continuation of the first mood begun in the
Moorings by the fire where we drank brandy. And you broke
a long silence (during which I feared we might be killed under
the road monsters travelling at high speed before and behind
us) to say that you would not and could not wait all your life,
that you would meet someone else and have a child by this
other man, this someone else, this nameless one.

Then, following another silence, staring grimly out the
smeared windscreen at the wake that the lorries were spewing
back at us, you said, No, you said, no indeed, you would not
wait. He would not show up. You would have no child by
him.

So we reached Wexford station and returned the mud-
caked car to Mylers (still *sans* apostrophe) and spoke to the
taciturn Banville and took the return train to Wicklow, and
all the Narbonne supporters had returned to Narbonne after
the dirty game in Lansdowne Road, the drawn game. So we
reached Wicklow station with frayed nerves, having splashed
out maybe £300, and walked down into the village for a last
drink at the Forge and I phoned up Sadie for a taxi and she
said she would be there in a jiffy.

Sadie Dolan was as good as her word and transported us
back to Ballymona Lodge. Dervorgilla was *in situ*, smiling a
cat's smirk (didn't we find the single bed a bit *cramped*?) and
loyal Blackie wagging his tail, delighted to have us back. The
bungalow shrank again as we walked in. Back we certainly
were with Blackie and the seven Dervorgillas.

32

Silent Love

Anastasia Ranoch lived at Oakmont Boulevard in Texas with two thoroughbred Skye terriers black and dusty like a pair of ambulatory hairy mats who spent their day barking through the fence at the grackles that infested the trees all tropical in the terrible Texas heat that came from the desert. These two and a male budgerigar called Martha who masturbated himself on a little plastic bell thoughtfully supplied by his mistress who walked barefoot about the house in slashed shorts as short as shorts could ever be, for Rory.

She had studied the Red Indians on graduating, had spent time in prison (trespass on a reservation), liked to dress in battle fatigues, and held the rank of major in President Reagan's secret army of PhD graduates specialising in a study of industrial diseases with findings perhaps useful for waging chemical warfare. She refused to let me see a photo of herself in uniform but could fly and travel at reduced rates if she wore it.

She looked very Russian in the photograph on her American passport. In strange hotels she kept a clasp-knife by her bed. She had had a bad experience in love.

On her last day at Ballymona Lodge she woke me at 8 a.m. to listen to a blackbird singing its heart out in Cooney's wood, a music that would have delighted Messiaen and delighted Rory and we made that which must not be spoken of (whisper it), were obliged to make t'nelis evol. Then we walked for the last time in the balmy air up the Columban Missionary avenue and were saluted by two nuns coming down from the convent.

The station was closed up but a Mohawk in black leather, leaning against the station wall, with a ring of spits about him, like a grasshopper evolving from the spittle, informed us that 'your man' – Hairy O'Hills – 'is somewhere up the line.' Michael Dolan, husband of Sadie, said he would drop your bags in later and we went for lunch in the Grand Hotel.

> Turkey and swedes
> Apple pie and ice-cream
> Coffee and Hennessy

An old Hitchcock movie *Young and Innocent* with Derrick de Marney was on in the public bar of the Leitrim where we had another Hennessy. The train left Wicklow at 5.05, reaching Connolly station 6.05.

Outside Bus Arus I left Anastasia for her dreadful long hike through space back to Oakmont Boulevard and the Skye terriers.

'Can't I cry now?'

> Dublin–Gatwick
> then Gatwick–Houston
> Houston–Austin

I took the next train back to Wicklow, feeling like a toad, watching a stupendous sunset over Kilcoole, phoned Sadie and was back in Ballymona Lodge by 7.30. A breast of turkey in the freezer, a bottle of Bordeaux a third depleted, and Dervorgilla snug abed in the mobile; at least the lights were off.

A fat bluebottle, eager for dung, lit on the wicker chair, flexed its hind legs briskly and flew out. I was wearing Anastasia's green socks; she had taken some pebbles from Magheramore back to her bedroom in Oakmont Boulevard as a memento, another bad experience in love.

Home to Texas!

Texas is home of strange allergies, and grackles, those coal-black Golgotha birds that can't sing and can hardly fly, but spend their time in the low thorn trees, shitting on the roofs of cars.

What is there to record of that time in May at Oakmont Boulevard? The fireflies in the Rose of Sharon bushes, the two Skye terrriers barking at passers-by behind the high fence, the death rattle of the grackles in the live-oak, the snail tracks on the fly-screen, the barometer climbing until it had registered 110 degrees in the midday shade, the hawks flying before the storm.

Black and dusty grackles cranked themselves across the sundrenched garden and I knocked one down with a rolled *New Yorker* that fell on the stiff pseudo-grass, the Astro-turf fouled by the terriers.

The Worst Choice

The worst choice of ales and beers in Europe is sold in Ireland at the highest prices. Over-refrigerated Budweiser, perhaps suitable for Texans in summer at temperatures of well over 100 degrees, is popular. Irish lager, like its English counterpart, is but a feeble imitation of the fine Pilsners brewed on the continent. Irish ale is weak and watery and full of gas, real ale unheard of.

Tommy Cullen has a shop at Brittas.

When four intruders waited in their car with the windows down, listening and waiting, he loaded his shotgun, crept down on the driver's side, put the barrel through the window and told the man, 'You have five seconds to get out of here.'

They took off over the roof.

No use feeling foolish if armed men break in and find you unarmed and defenceless. Tommy keeps the shotgun under his bed. The area around Brittas is all firearms, burglar alarms and guard-dogs, as you can find out at night, when the prowlers are abroad, setting off the guard dogs and the alarms.

Blackie goes a-roaming again. Roaming the roads will be the death of that dog. What's the significance of the big black dog that follows the traveller everywhere?

Davis and Demons

The young pine wood that the dead Cooney had planted as his memorial makes its sounds all night, bird-call and breeze, the risen wind batters it, the poachers pass through unseen with their silent dogs. Retired to bed with windows closed behind the venetian blinds I am not thinking of ghosts and demons of the night but of flesh and blood raiders masked in balaclavas and armed with shotguns who come in cars to coast silently over the cattle-trap and arrive at my doorstep; a blow of a crowbar and they are in. Blackie is knocked on the head.

Sanguineous bugaboos move by night in stolen cars and all those who sleep the sleep of the just are their allotted prey.

The guard-dogs bark all night. Any suspicious noise on the road brings Blackie out of his kennel to bay; and he sets off the others, beginning with Dr Meenan's dog; a chain reaction gets dogs barking as far as Herbst's yard and beyond.

Last December in Santa Cruz the seals lay about the pier and barked all night like dogs when I was making free of the Suchmans' drinks cabinet at four in the morning, playing Bach sonatas for violin and harpsichord, No. 5 in F Minor for preference, listening to the seals barking.

Dervorgilla's binoculars pulled the valley and distant line of hills closer. An almost Bavarian landscape was revealed on this lovely summer's day with the patio woodwork creaking in

the sun, jackdaws scoffing in a tod of ivy and the first swallows
of summer spurting by after rising insects. Why is it one takes
the summer days of other countries for granted but never an
Irish summer? Is it because they are so rare? The prancing air
of Cape Town with outsize swallows flying over the harbour,
the High Rand day of Johannesburg where I lived for two
years, the dry heat of a Karoo winter's day, sandy Prussian day
of Berlin, Bavarian day in Munich with the *Föhn* blowing, the
Copenhagen day and Andalusian day all were known to Rory
in his years of travel. But Irish summers were strange and
unexpected and only the summers of my distant youth (1933)
seemed fixed and abiding. The changing countryside and its
changing people were unfamiliar and outlandish as Reykjavik
or Watseka, Illinois.

Clinton Binnions is putting up electrified wire in his field,
to define the grazing grounds of his sportful Friesians that
have never known of the slaughterhouse and cavort about,
butting each other and pretending to be alarmed by Ned
Ward's white setter who runs at them in mock attacks. Have
the Friesians infected Clinton with their skittishness or has he
infected them with his? Ireland's only swimming farmer.

Sunday, 30 June
Cycled back from Brittas with Blackie weaving all over the
road to find a note from brother scratched with key on silver-
foil of cigarette papers.

> I will call at about 9 a.m. tomorrow
> in case you need a lift to the station.
> I think it is tomorrow you go to see
> the King? Colum.

Nelsons came for dinner. Dorothy's cat face, beatific smile of
pure exhaustion, pale and overworked. They are saving to
buy a semi-detached house in the vale of Shanganagh.
Trouble with publisher Cashman, working on second novel.
Hot Dublin scandal: woman at hen party found herself last in

line for powder-room. Famous lesbian was pleasuring all who
came, in a queue, gratifications digital or oral. Schsshters!

Myths begin in Ireland as shaggy dog stories; famous
(though perfectly ordinary) personalities become legendary
beings. Perfectly ordinary individuals in the entertainment,
sports and communications trade became regular folk heroes
overnight, names to conjure with; famous almost by accident,
become legendary beings. O'Hehir the sports broadcaster
with his frantic soprano screeching, affable Gabo, moanin'
low Bono and the Band-Aid man Geldof, all pure buffoons in
their various ways, as tall, white-bearded Noel Purcell before
them. Since nothing much could be said in their favour they
were elevated to the lofty status of Great Irishmen of Our
Time.

In a derelict three-storey house overlooking the river on
Leitrim Place near the pub lives bachelor Davis. His condition
appears to be one of extreme destitution; he shuffles about in
a greasy overcoat, his gooseberry eyes watering, grey arthritic
hands ingrained with old dirt. Yet the Davis family were well-
off once; he drove the first motor car through Wicklow. He
lives alone, a needy bachelor; the house was broken into and
the family silver stolen. Behind a high untended hedge Davis
lives out what remains of his life; you would take him for a
tramp.

I crossed the river by the low bridge, saw crabs tumbling
past with the outgoing tide; and so by the yard of empty
Guinness barrels, iron lungs waiting to be collected from
Dowlings riverside hostelry.

In the Leitrim Bar I am civilly served a shot of Jameson by
the redheaded son of the former butcher who has two shops
on the main street. Looking out the window I see the sea
breaking over the low wall and the shell of the old station, its
platform and loading sheds long disused, where I had arrived
for a week's holiday around 1949. The station had moved
inland since; it had stood there once with the solid look of
permanancy peculiar to railway stations, when I stepped off
the train, aged about twenty-one years. In an August heat

wave Conal ('Bruiser') Cullinane and I paddled over the horizon. We could see fathoms down into the clear green sea.

You can look at something a hundred times and not recognise it: namely, the ruins of a railway station long abandoned by the sea.

35

The King and Queen of Spain

Monday, 1 July

Ned called at 8.20 a.m., brother Colum at 9.15 to take me to the station (the County Council offices being just down the hill). The gold-edged invitation card from the Department of Foreign Affairs stated that

> The Taoiseach and Mrs Fitzgerald request the pleasure of your company at lunch in the Iveagh House at 1.00 p.m. in honour of Their Majesties the King and Queen of Spain on the occasion of their visit to Ireland.
> P.M. Informal dress.

In my case very informal. The only suitable apparel I possessed was at the cleaners, an Aran baínín jacket dyed black, sans buttons and lapels, a present from a man in Shamley Green, Surrey.

I had seen a jacket in the window of a high-class haberdashery in Kildare Street opposite Dáil Éireann. Slip it on, said the suave outfitter, who praised the fit and hang, as good as tailored, made for me. He was prepared to knock a fiver off the retail price; so I made out a cheque for £100, thrice the price I had ever paid for a jacket, this one of handwoven Donegal tweed. Colours from our countryside. Joy and health to you when you wear this, said the weaver's tag. I said I would keep it on.

A crowd of idlers had gathered about Iveagh House and gardai and plainclothes detectives were positioned along the railings of Stephen's Green; for the state visit of the Spanish royals was common knowledge since they had appeared the previous evening on *Today Tonight* TV bulletin and had been introduced to an enchanted nation by Mr Brian Farrell, constricted in dinner jacket and bow-tie.

They had already paid a courtesy visit to President Hillery at Arus an Uachtaran in the Phoenix Park and exchanged pleasantries about the climate. King Juan Carlos then made a long speech in Spanish out of which emerged, as flotsam on the flood, *Irlanda, España, Armada, Iglesia, Americana*; to all of which Queen Sofia listened attentively, smiling sweetly when she deemed it appropriate. Toasts to both nations were proposed and drunk.

Going in in my camouflage I was among men in dark suits and stout elderly priests in black standing by the bar with drinks in hand amiably chatting with all the aplomb of men of the world accustomed to such formal occasions when clergy and laity commingled pleasantly as the gin and tonic in their fists.

State visits and cultural events flush out the pushier type of prelate, as sporting events always flush out a rash of priests to take the best seats as their God-given right or throw in the ball at Gaelic games and then present cups to the victors as smoothly as they offer ciborium and consecrated host to the faithful with their tongues out for it. Standing on windy hillsides at coursing matches they cheer on the greyhounds and watch them tear the hares asunder; as if there were a close kinship between the May altar and processions and rituals in the open air and the GAA and blood sports in general, accepted as an appropriately healthy and natural masculine sort of activity fit for strapping Gaels of all stripes.

The stout elderly and now thoroughly flushed clerics who stood by the serving hatch were no doubt former Salamanca novices who after ordination had got up into the pulpit to preach Franco's cause against Godless Communism. They congregated in the bar as though such lay premises were familiar as their own sacristies. Such processions and rituals had been going on in Ireland ever since the Eucharistic Congress in 1932.

I questioned a flunkey as to the correct protocol for addressing the King. 'Your Majesty.' Pure gold! The clang of sword unsheathed, the taunting challenge, lances upraised against a blue sky, pennants aflutter. Lucia Joyce doted on the weak Windsors, would jump on any bus bound for Windsor, wrote to the King of England: 'Majesty.'

There would be no delay; just a quick handshake and pass along into the dining room where place-cards were on every table.

Never had I been presented to royalty before, much less shaken the hand of a King and his Queen. This one did not require to dress up to be a King. In his hand he held no sceptre, on his head there was no crown, about his shoulders no ermine-lined cape festooned with medals; yet his whole appearance was manifestly kingly. This was the Spanish King who had marched alone into the Cortes already assembled and informed his Generals that the Putsch was off; they should remember their oaths of loyalty to him. They could go home.

The winding reception line went down a short flight of carpeted stairs and rose again on the far side, where the royal pair would presently appear with the Fitzgeralds. Mrs Fitzgerald smiled from her wheelchair as though it were perfectly natural to smile up from a wheelchair to a gathering of stout elderly priests lining up to shake the kingly hand and look humbly into his eye, encounter that parboiled Bourbon stare. Mr Haughey, former Taoiseach and now Leader of the Opposition, was immediately ahead of me in his double vents, always smaller than expected, blowing his nose with circumspection into a spotless linen handkerchief. Ahead of him shuffled the old priests who had studied in Salamanca and sided for the Roman Catholic Church and Christ and their Order and Franco.

And now Mr Haughey had reached the King and did not

'make a leg' but bowed his head as if receiving holy communion and I heard his low deferential murmur as he took
the King's hand. Then I was face to face with the King. I had
written that he looked constipated on the Spanish stamps; for
such *lèse-majesté* one could end up in the stocks. But had el
Rey Juan Carlos I read it? Beneath the immensely high
Bourbon forehead the eyes of a keen yachtsman stared at me.

'*Su Majestad*,' I murmured, timidly pressing the King's
hand. And then to Queen Sofia: '*Su Majestad*.'

'You've forgotten me,' said an amused voice from below as
a gracious hand was extended from the wheelchair.

'No, I haven't,' I lied, and reeled on, propelled by the
elderly priests now made ravenous by rich cooking aromas,
into the high-ceiling chamber miraculously fragrant, a place
as cool as the Alhambra with a breeze blowing through. I was
seated at a table with the political correspondent of the *Irish
Times* and a Cistercian monk who was editor of *Crux*.

The menu had ingeniously amalgamated the colours of the
two flags. A gazpacho soup, turbot and chillies with new Irish
potatoes, chilled Spanish white wine, a sorbet with coffee and
cognac, and you would not get as good at Restaurante
Hermanos Macias in Ronda. The King sipped red wine and
stared thoughtfully away into space, no doubt going over the
lines of his speech, staring over the heads of the old priests
now lashing into the good fare; the high-domed forehead
dominated the table. Garrett Fitzgerald was charming Queen
Sofia who was laughing. Then the Taoiseach stood up and
made a speech in fluent Spanish not once consulting notes; to
which King Juan Carlos responded in stilted English.

The priests applauded. Mumm champagne was served up
and the dining room stood for toasts: Spain and Ireland, the
King and Queen. The battle of Kinsale was tactfully avoided;
whereupon the royals departed. Equerries were already
packing, flight times checked; the royal entourage was
heading west. The *Irish Times* man and I finished off the
Mumm. It had been a splendid luncheon party.

36

The *Camarero* Miguel Lopez Rojas

You do not presume to pester or bother a King with idle questions, much less volunteer information or engage in backchat; one does not question Kings, who have no tactful responses to such impertinence. If he should come calling to your house *you* stand.

I had wanted to tell the King that at least one of his subjects – Miguel who worked long hours in the Bar Alhambra in Nerja – was on his feet from ten in the morning until two the next; had been his loyal subject years before he had ascended the throne.

One fine summer morning in Nerja I was having coffee and cognac when there came the throbbing of mighty engines passing close in to the Balcon de Europa. Stepping out into the heat I saw the immaculately white and spick and span destroyer bristling with long-barrelled guns passing close in as if to warn or impress the watchers. The entire ship's company in white were drawn up ramrod stiff on deck, saluting the flag, hands and faces brown as teak, come perhaps from Alicante or Cartagena and now heading in for Málaga.

Franco the fox dared not come all the way from his lair in Madrid, not on the high winding road from Almería for it became progressively more dangerous and could be mined or blocked with dynamite, and man–made avalanches send motorcades into the sea. For the last leg of the journey he was coming by sea, out of sight in his air-conditioned cabin. The dictator who had made Hitler wait and kick his heels while he took his siesta was a small, portly, choleric man who nursed his phlebitis, took his pills, nursed memories of north Africa and the Rif, the fight for Malaga and perhaps the names of those executed by his orders.

I told Miguel that the Caudillo was passing. By way of dismissive response he narrowed his eyes and spat in the dust.

All dictators have this in common: they take little mincing steps, fussy as goats. Perhaps their jackboots are killing them?

37

Epistolary: 1974–78

I have come upon some letters my brother wrote me eleven years ago when he was living at Three Mile Water, before Dunganstown East. He wrote to me from the wilds of Wicklow, where he was digging himself in.

> CULLEN COTTAGE
> THREE MILE WATER
> NEAR WICKLOW
>
> 14 Oct. 1974

Dear Rory,

A few lines, as promised.

Shall I begin it? Now actually 14th Dec. Time did not permit a second line until now. Working like shit in the office & in my own time on office work to the detriment of my own affairs,. I work late in the evenings & rarely have a lunch hour with the result that I calculate I work a six day week for the price of five. It's daft. Why do I do it? To avoid falling below a certain minimum level of incompetence I do both my own work & that of my three 'assistants,' who I, in fact, assist. I got rid of one, psychopathic as well as incompetent, who wouldn't do what he was asked, but not for that reason but only by saying either he left or I did. (Back to Ludlow Road, or worse – charming prospect.) Although any reasonable organisation would have been glad of the opportunity to get such a person out, this character was simply passed on to someone else eventually, the first two on whom it was tried declining. So all the architects have to contend with this & adopt the attitude of not having the staff so that the work can't be done, generally concentrating on their own affairs, owning pubs & chemist shops about the city & drawing £4,000 a year; which is a great pity as the work is useful & pleasant & simple enough to be capable of being done without any assistants, but there is so much of it that it takes a lot of time & I keep struggling to get on top of it, which is in theory possible but I can never quite achieve.

I have brought home work this weekend & was up until 3 & 4 o'clock last weekend. The purchase of the land for the house is complete but there is no opportunity to design it. I suspect, incidentally, that it was bought just too soon & prices are now going down . . .

CULLEN COTTAGE
THREE MILE WATER
NEAR WICKLOW

30 March 1978

Dear Rory,

So that is where you are (wherever it is), if you are still there?* I have not verified your position on the map. I would do so if there was any chance of going in that direction; but there is not, as my house building struggles continue & do not show much evidence of coming to an end. I can, perhaps, see a minimum that could be done to make it habitable, at which point we could move in & finish the rest afterwards. It is not how I would have liked to go about it, but probably that will happen. It is necessary to move in at a certain stage to prevent the interior fittings being stolen. However as it is a considerable minimum & I work slowly I could not say when this might be. I am in the difficult position of knowing, perhaps too well, how things should be in theory without having any practical experience of how to carry them out in practice. I remember seeing Werner Schurmann building his house & thinking I could never attempt such a thing, but am doing all right, as far as it goes. At the moment I am still only at the stage of taking down & rebuilding defective work which I paid local cowboys to do, & this is more tedious than building it in the first place. They were unable to make an opening of the correct size for a door frame or window frame, leaving gaps of up to two inches which they were unable to fill in such a way as to keep out the rain. The roof also leaks, for which I have myself to blame because although I knew there was such a thing as an exposed site I did not take it very seriously, assuming that a fairly steep roof pitch would shed water in any circumstances. Unfortunately the site is probably more in the category of very exposed, being elevated & by the sea, & the rain is capable of being driven from the eaves up the roof & over the ridge rather than flowing downwards in the manner one would expect. When driven like this for a day or so in a gale it can find its way in if there are any mistakes. I have come to detest the wind, which has also blown scaffolding off the roof, breaking rooflights, & taking nine square feet of aluminium sheet off the top of the chimney & left it in a ditch a quarter of a mile away.

All of which is very tiresome in every sense. When not working I sleep, & then insufficiently. I received a copy of your book, with thanks, but my only reading these days is the paper, during meals, & so out of touch that of the two works you mention as influences I have not even heard. Therefore, as a paper reader, I have seen & enjoyed your pieces on Ireland. They are vivid & exact, such as the pipers like 'demented bees,' a description which is quite audible. Also Ben Kiely's praise of the introduction to the short story anthology, which I would like to see some time. Cuttings, as always, are enclosed, possibly of no interest except the obituary of Heidegger to which I draw your attention with reference to my remarks about his influence on Beckett: Being can be addressed not expressed, waited for (!) not spoken for . . . that seems clear enough?

C.

* I was sharing a house, a model Irish cottage, with Rosita at Beladangan across the causeway in Iar Connaught.

DUNGANSTOWN EAST
WICKLOW

13 July 1978
Thursday

Dear Rory,

Thank you for yours of 22 May. Is it such a time ago? It seems like a few weeks. These long Summer days seem shorter than the others. I go in the garden after dinner, presently it is after 11 & another day is gone without much to show except a lot of grass cut. This year I determined to cut it before the seed had a chance to form since neglecting it in the last few years for house painting with the result that even the vegetable patches were attempting to revert to their natural state, which is that of a meadow rather than a garden. I have been cutting our meadow with a scythe, or half an acre of it, a pleasant occupation when the swing of it is acquired, which has taken me a few years & I now fly along like a character from a bad novel by John McGahern. I suppose what is wrong with him is what Marinetti objected to: '. . . memory, nostalgia, the fog of legend produced by remoteness in time, the exotic fascination produced by remoteness in space, the picturesque, the imprecise, rusticity, wild solitude, corrosion, multicoloured disorder, twilight shadows, weariness, the soiled traces of the years, the crumbling of ruins, the taste of decay, pessimism, phthisis, suicide, the blandishments of pain, the aesthetics of failure.'

Hoping you own ills have gone away.

C.

Rather than face the boredom of driving his Mini on motorways across England my brother took the side roads and by-ways into Wales, heading for the Holyhead ferry. He fell asleep at the wheel and crashed. It was a bad crash out of which he was lucky to come alive. This was some years before when I was living in London.

He wrote to me from a hospital in Wales. Later, on the mend but still on crutches, he summoned me into Wales to get him out of hospital and we travelled back by train, and then took a bus to his hutch in Ealing where he insisted on cooking lunch.

Assembling the components of this dull but nutritious meal (we were spared cabbage) my brother sailed about the kitchen on his new crutches with all the nonchalance and *élan* of those intrepid early aviators who flew channels and oceans as if they were mere ditches. As if he had been doing this all his life; as in a sense he had, and overcoming all obstacles by sheer obstinacy. His resourcefulness, like his patience, was endless. All his life he had consumed stewed apples and Bird's custard for the motions and Swiss rolls for a treat; which was another form of constancy, of loyalty to his obligations, his life.

Colum and Stella Veronica returned to Ireland along the motorway in their Tin Lizzie and my brother had his hands clawed off by one of the wild Russian cats rescued from the building sites, who did not care to travel in a Mini box.

38

The Dodo in London

In those trying times my estranged wife Jane and I were cooped up on the fifth or topmost floor of a five-room walk-up cold-water rent-controlled apartment above shops on Muswell Hill Broadway in north London.

Our flat was the highest of the highest building on the highest hill surmounted by a little tower overlooking Alexandra Park and the Palace, adjoining an ABC cinema complex that was later demolished.

The ceiling of the flat immediately below us was leaking and then systematically pulled down by a clever Cockney, until it was on the living-room floor and the landlord liable for repairs. After twenty years of ding-dong our marriage was coming to an end; as were many others in a building always leaking and in need of running and immediate repairs.

In the hazy blue distance lay Potters Bar in Hertfordshire, Hatfield and the way north. The kindergarten and Mrs Kanji was just below; a fifteen-minute bus ride took my middle lad to Barnet Art College and beyond that Havendon Wood and open countryside, a haven for lechers in the wheatfields.

From the wrought-iron balcony at the rear you could see down to the playing fields of Crouch End and the noble dome of St Paul's.

A landing covered in a threadbare runner bisected the apartment from front door to bathroom in the back; the rooms led off this, three narrow bedrooms, a more commodious master bedroom, and a living room lined with books that overlooked the Broadway and its incessant traffic.

There the Dodo, not seen in years, paid us an unexpected flying visit, travelling by train from Largs on the Firth of Clyde. I had not set eyes on this odd relinquent of mine since our mother's demise in Dun Laoghaire some years before, when he had flitted in and out, not attending the funeral as he thought it might be too distressing for his finer sensibilities.

To what now did we owe this singular honour? *Tiens!* He just happened to be passing through *en route* to Paris and needed a place to lay his weary head for the night, and what could be more natural than to beg a favour of his younger brother? He had phoned my wife to ask whether we could put him up for the night; and she could hardly refuse him. It was high time he paid us a visit; the lads must have grown big as trees.

When I heard the buzzer go I pressed the release button and a disembodied distant voice squawked down below amid the din of the Broadway that swelled in a crescendo as he pushed open the street door and now he was coming up. I opened the apartment door and waited for him to appear, not having seen him in seventeen years.

The bloody old Dodo was coming up, the old rip, a rare visitant indeed; I was curious to see how Time had dealt with him. He halted at the mezzanine below, rang the bell, cleared his throat; the door was opened by Mrs Fisher and my brother addressed her in that unforgettable fluty mooing voice without maleness or resolution or lung-power in it; an odd buttery, neutered voice on the stairs, a whispery gush of sibilants.

'Does Mr Rory live here by any chance?'

Top floor, boss! Go right up! Right on, squire! They're in!

Breathing stealthily through his wide-winged nostrils the Dodo slowly ascended the last flight of uncarpeted stairs that stank of dog piss (the Barraddas yappers), grasping in his right hand a golf driver without its covering. He appeared from the waist up, had grown corpulent and was now a veritable

Mycroft Holmes in girth, wearing well-cut expensive tweed suiting of grouse-moor twill.

He had the face of a Roman emperor, a fleshly face set into its final form – an odd mixture of my father's weak face and my mother's in a certain mood. This would be his final face, the visage he would take with him into the grave. He had brought no presents; had he not brought himself all the way from far distant Largs, a perilous journey southward! Step in, step in, whoever you are.

He bore no malice, shook no hands. He entered nodding as if he knew us well and had come here many times before and been welcomed as a true and valued friend.

The Dodo perched himself on the very edge of the sofa and accepted a gin and tonic, holding the driver like a mace between his knees. He was heavy and monumental as a graven image; a non-smoker he could remain silent without any embarrassment. He was puffed after the climb, one hand masterfully reposing on his knee, The Great Condottiere.

Who spoke of the density that people seem to possess as we keenly observe them? He kept his eye fixed on me, his mother's hazel eyes alight with some secret mischief (her humour had always been rather bitter), enjoying some private joke which I couldn't share. His head wobbled on its broad axis. This was his easygoing social manner; he was at his ease in any company, among the golfers at Largs where he was regarded as 'quite a local celebrity'.

Was he intending to play golf in Paris with one club? And were the partners or partner male or female?

When supper was announced he marched to the table in the kitchen with measured tread, always a good trencherman.

My sons were in stitches; they had not expected such a strange uncle. He consumed his *babotjie* with a steady and methodical chomping, and when the meal was over announced that now he was off to the West End; he had booked a seat for a play. He was flying on to Paris in the morning; at what hour did we rise?

Next morning I took him to the bus stop. Adieu, happy

landings, keep the head down, watch that shank. He shook all over to indicate silent mirth as he stepped aboard the W7 for Finsbury Park and was whirled off down the hill. I hoped that was the end of him. He had never been much of an older brother to me. Indeed nothing fraternal existed between myself and that cold slab I call the Dodo.

39

The Classic Cinema
in Baker Street

Coming out of the Classic cinema into the gloaming, the late afternoon summer light peculiar to Baker Street and the purlieus of Madame Tussaud's — there was a pleasant pub opposite that I occasionally frequented — who do you suppose I saw strolling ahead in black leather jacket but Lindsay Anderson, and walking behind him my brother, unknown to each other, the last two people I would have thought to see there but the two most likely to travel distances to see a Welles movie, particularly *The Magnificent Ambersons*.

In those far-off days before marriage I was working in an extrusion moulding plant in Burnt Oak and reading Sartre's *Nausea* over lunch (two thin pork chops and tinned peas) in a transport café on the Great North Road. I introduced my brother to Anderson and they repaired to a coffee joint on Marylebone Road. I took a bus going south to the Bayswater Road, then another going west to Notting Hill Gate, then the Central Line tube going to Ealing Common via White City, still full of the strange emotions that the movie had evoked.

I had first seen *Citizen Kane* with Philomena Rafferty in a repertory cinema near Marble Arch; my brother, ever contrary, dismissed it as a young man showing off. But what showing off. He professed to be an admirer of *The Great Gatsby*, the novel not the movie; a novel about 'the huge incoherent failure of a house' and a dream (Daisy).

Welles had died working at his desk late on the night of Wednesday, 9 October a few hours after Old Parr and I would set off downhill into the pitch darkness, followed by the curses of the mad Finn. Two years later his ashes would be flown to Malaga in an unmarked blue urn in the safe keeping of Beatrice Welles, his daughter by Rita Hayworth; to be immured in a wall on the bull-farm of his *amigo* Antonio Ordoñez near Ronda. An unmarked urn set into a brick wall without a plaque marks his last and most secret resting place, perhaps known only to Ordoñez.

Twenty or more years previously I had watched him (Ordoñez) working the bulls in a *corrida* with Jaime Ostos and El Viti in the bullring by the Alameda Gardens. Years on I lunched at the Restaurante Hnos. Macias (*Un Tipico Rincon Rodeño en un Marco Incomparable*) with my last love Alannah near the Ronda bullring. Our waiter said that Ordoñez had semi-retired but was still killing the bulls; it was in his blood. One of his old picadors had been in the previous night to take a bowl of soup.

Orson Welles's Xanadu – Hearst's San Simeon – was the frightening castle of a fairy tale, with its hall of mirrors, its echoing corridors and wide flights of shadowy stairs, its fireplace the size of a barn, the wifely boudoir a doll's room, the inmates shrinking away, observed coldly by the sinister butler who knew where all the bodies were buried.

A strange clear late afternoon light even at 8.00 p.m. on 6 June 1972, my sons kicking football on the patch below the flats, brother Colum in Carmarthen West Wales general hospital. Rather than go on the motorway he took side roads into Wales, fell asleep at the wheel, crashed into a wall, came to hearing a South African voice asking for an ambulance; he had a broken leg, jaw and teeth and is now on crutches. He comes by train to London tomorrow, wishes me to accompany him from Wales.

Muted whirr of the pet hamster on its treadmill down the corridor and a recorded voice in my ear explains in German that all the lines into West Berlin are overloaded. A dry whirring in my ear as the phone rings in an empty flat in Schwabing.

40

Mornings in the Dewy Dell

In my years in Muswell Hill I drank in the pubs around there and in Highgate village or walked through Highgate Wood and Ken Wood and Hampstead Heath to the various pubs of Hampstead to Harry's bar on the hill, the Coach & Groom.

V. S. Pritchett says that you can knock on any second door in London and find people there who have travelled the world, and I have found this to be true of casual acquaintances encountered in pubs. Morning drinkers in London always have interesting stories to tell, taste buds lubricated and tongues loosened by the first pint of the day, *memoria technica* clicking into action.

One fine summer morning I descended the fire escape and got on to the pathway that joins Alexandra Park and Highgate Wood, formerly a railway line, now the dewy dell, and made my way to the rustic Royal Oak, a Courage house deserted at that hour. Presently an unshaven geezer came in and immersed himself in the *Daily Mirror*, with the first foaming pint of the day to hand, best bitter a thirst-quencher with salted peanuts.

I read in the *Guardian* that the headless corpse of a man had been found sitting bolt upright in the passenger seat of an architect's car parked opposite the main gates of Highgate cemetery. On his way to work the architect had seen something peculiar on the nearside seat, which at first he took to be a log of wood put there for a joke; but when he got into the car he found a male corpse minus the head, apparently removed from a coffin in the nearby cemetery. But why leave it in his car? Why dig it up anyway? Why remove the head?

More morning drinkers began to file into the public bar for jovial banter. I fell into conversation with a ruddy-faced dapper little man who introduced himself as Geoffrey Hogg late of Norwich and the Norfolk Fusiliers (were they the famous Buffs?), the father of six bouncing daughters, an admirer of the poetry of George Herbert and the music of Elgar.

'Trooping the Colour is based on illiteracy. Even so I could cheerfully wake up each morning to the strains of a military band.'

Here the amiable Hogg gave a strange high-pitched laugh. I wondered whether he was by any chance related to the man who had wanted to or had cuckolded Shelley but didn't think it proper to enquire. Perhaps he was. He told me that he had lost a translation of Luther's *Table Talk* in the Great Yarmouth flood. We spoke of Charles Lamb and his attempts to give up smoking, both he and Coleridge threw their pipes away on Hampstead Heath, when it was country, returning next morning to look for them. We spoke of De Quincey and his drug addiction.

'Did you read about that corpse found in the car in Highgate?' I asked. 'I wonder who put it there.'

'That would be Farrant up to his tricks. He drinks in the Prince of Wales with the Welsh witch. When we were intro-duced by Darcey Farcey he gave me a most peculiar handshake. A sort of manual French kiss.'

'That would be Farrant.'

Nothing could put a dampener on Geoffrey Hogg late of the Buffs; he fairly exuded sound common sense.

The loan imbiber in the Alexandra had been a film pro-jectionist in Mozambique. He told me that when the natives couldn't pay their taxes, Salazar had sent out his bombers from Portugal and bombed the village, having warned them to get out; he wanted to teach them a salutary lesson. They came in with their taxes. Salazar had put manners on them. 'Well, you can't run a dictatorship along humanitarian lines.'

Had I not been there with the puppets, come by road from rainy Blantyre out of what was Rhodesia; crossed the Zambesi at Tet, saw a monkey chained on a platform in a yard at evening, discovered that sparkling Portuguese rosé in the bubble-shaped bottle with the decorative label. Mateus Rosé, a good name for some profiteering lecher. Mateus Rosé cost ten and sixpence, or two for a guinea. In the days when newspapers cost a penny, a gin and tonic half a crown and there were eight in a pound, a quid.

Those were the days when Jane and I lived high up on Muswell Hill Broadway; when I couldn't extract royalties from a tight-fisted publisher; when our marriage had begun to break up; when I drank like a fish and my work went off the rails.

41

The Finn

In early October of that year I had a visitor staying. Testy Old Parr arrived from over the Irish Sea for a short winter break, dossing down in the mobile home in the paddock, filing the chain off Dervorgilla's bicycle, for which I would have to stump up £5 later. We cycled to McDaniel's for a drink.

Dole boys were bashing balls about the two snooker tables that were rarely unoccupied and a gross spillage of lurid colours and stereophonic dialogue spewed from a monster TV screen raised on high. The place was commodious as an aircraft hangar and as unappealing. As we seated ourselves in the ingle, John Stamp took an armful of elongated wedges of dried turf and piled them up into a great conflagration under the stuffed fox that stared down with blind glassy eyes. You had the choice of being roasted in the ingle or frozen by the counter.

John brought us hot whiskies and halves of Guinness. A leering hairy lank fellow came to sit opposite us, sniggering into his drink, presently identifying himself as a Finn, and certainly an unsober one, disposed to be offensive. I had no wish to bandy words with this sallow fellow nodding into his drink. He had reached the stage of insobriety where he wanted to be offensive and presently had dismissed us with contempt as bourgeois and even – compounding the insult –

petit bourgeois. He invited us to step outside.

No thanks.

As we left we heard him phoning the Garda barracks in Wicklow. We took off without lights into the pitch darkness, soaring off down the long hill. I took my bearings from the faint starlight that showed between the trees not meeting overhead. Old Parr followed.

Drunker than skunks, veritable bats out of Hell, pedalling madly fit to beat the demented cyclist racing the express train in Jarry's *Supermale*, down we plunged headlong into the dangerous darkness below.

Next morning we were on the road again, tyres pumped up, heading for Lil Doyle's, turkey sandwiches and gin.

In the afternoon as darkness was falling we entered Healy's pub in Wicklow town and were set upon by a local drunk who became even more abusive than the Finn. He enquired where our yacht was moored. He said he would take it offa us; he was going to take everything offa us. He took us for Englishmen, I in my Blue Peter and Old Parr, who was certainly an Englishman (but with an Irish mother from Ballina), born in India.

Old Parr swirled his Guinness about in the glass to bring up a head, but offered no comment, staring sagaciously at the row of bottles confronting him. His tufted grey locks were standing on end as though he had seen an apparition.

'The same again?'

'Why not.'

42

'Cash' Up for Sentencing

'Didn't Cash get off light,' said Ned Ward.
'How's that?'
'A thirty quid fine is nothing to Cash.'

Cash Murphy had appeared briefly in court to answer charges, to be fined a very nominal amount by a lenient Justice of the Peace and given several months in which to pay it. The Guards said that Cash's house was a regular Ali Baba's cave of nicked property, among which were Ann Lait's car-parts and Dervorgilla's cushions. His defence had been a barefaced lie; his mammy *wasn't* dying.

A few days later I passed him on the steps leading from the butcher's shop to the harbour where a freighter from Bilbao waited to take on a cargo of timber.

Out of great misery comes great joy. Dervorgilla's cushions were returned to their rightful owner and the covers thrown straight into the washing machine which thundered away day and night on its rotors. She had insisted that the place be kept in apple-pie order and would not agree to Biddy cleaning once a week as I had suggested. She had backed away from me as from a leper when I approached smoking a roll-up; all the rooms but mine were non-smoking areas.

43

Year Ending

Clinton Binnions advances slowly in green wellingtons amid his placidly grazing herd of Friesians who hardly deign to take notice of him as he strolls among them, slaps a meaty hindquarter ('Thou art mine, goodly lass!'). The sea-swimmer, horse-rider, tennis player who makes his own wine now claps his hands; and slowly they rise up and amble off stage, swishing their tails. Binnions, abstracted, hands plunged in pockets, his thoughts far away, follows them off the field.

I was thinking today that my father, dead these sixteen years, was like one of those minor Shakespearean characters – Rosencrantz and Guildenstern – who are killed offstage and never rejoin the action but take a curtain call at the end when they appear half out of character (already actors on their way home), bowing deeply to the audience, with complacent smiles.

Saw a rare thing on tonight's RTE station: a Finnish film on Elias Lönnrot. Reindeer pull a sledge at top speed across the snow-plain, a cabin full of wild dancing girls throwing up their skirts to expose naughty linen petticoats. Doesn't he figure in one of Borge's fables as a figure of doom?

Made sortie out for wood. Phone rang twice; I did not answer. Dervorgilla is due mid-September, has been away since Sunday, 23 June. Her mail has already begun to accumulate. An thinking of moving on when she returns. A van goes by, on the side is inscribed SADIE DOLAN.

I recall Paddy Collins in his dark den in Delgany gate lodge near the Bell Hole, abuzz with house flies thickly clustered. He said they didn't bother him, he quite liked them, as company. He made trips to Dublin on the bus to relieve the monotony; was lionised by the ladies in the Arts Club. 'It's Paddy!'

Crusty epistle from Old Parr rusticating in France, where Massif Central will find him. 'Abandoned language almost entirely, took to hand signs, rubbing belly, tipping thumb towards the mouth. Swimming in lakes, wine-tasting. Parry is bound for the Great Barrier Reef.'

25 September (Yom Kippur)

Woke before alarum with finger on stop button. Ambitious young David Hockney had tacked cautionary precept above his bed, for his eyes alone to see as he woke: *Get Up Immediately!* Seems to have worked in his case. Motion in shed as kettle boils, out of delicacy for sleeper whose bedroom abuts on bathroom. Mist obscures valley almost to door. Both windows wide open, post van brings mail for sleeper.

Ned Ward came at midday to say Gardai had told him that farmer had shot a bitch and her two ever-straying pups who had been worrying his sheep. Dervorgilla on her back on sofa engaged in long telephone conversation. She goes into hospital tomorrow.

30 September

Phoned Stevens Hospital and got on to Dervorgilla. Operation tomorrow, she needs transistor and Chopin piano tapes. Convalescence with the Grennans.

Ned went to see corpse of setter bitch and pups shot a week ago. Pheasant shooting season begins tomorrow.

2 October

Biddy called with clinging daughter Lara with thumb in mouth in company of little Siobhan Herbst, with exophthalmic eyes and brown skin, sister of little Orson Herbst. Biddy screeching 'Mind your new dress!' to fractious daughter, on her worst behaviour.

Phoned Stevens Hospital. Dervorgilla sounded weak, requires roll of film.

3 October

Dental appointment. Mini crashes over cattle-trap, flurry of gravel and crunch of brakes. The brother!

'I've only got ten minutes to spare!'

Accepts glass of chilled white wine, chomping at his sandwiches, always the same, then rushes me to Matthews's surgery.

Afterwards to Periwinkle for hot toddy and cloves. Fug of tobacco fumes and TV hubbub. Asked for it to be turned down and I would accept a second hot toddy. Boozer with purple face, scum of Guinness on lips, wipes lips with back of hairy hand, staring fixedly at me, then up at TV screen, its racket moderated.

'Izzy n'Amorican or whah? Ah fukkim!'

Brother takes two gins and lime, then off to dig in garden; his compost heap needs some attention. He allows himself little free time but finds it refreshing to dig after a long day in the County Council office.

He is famous for his refusal to accept bribes.

4 October

Another dental appointment at 2.00 p.m. Downpour woke me at 4.00 a.m. Lightning over hills, moon scudding through clouds. Storm reaches crescendo, abates, then comes again. I lie listening, comatose, warm and secure as Cooney's wood is buffeted by gale for an hour. Late for appointment.

Recalling (under the needle, to piped Muzak) Stella's unlikely account of her dental appointment 'at nine' in Westland Row some years ago. She wondered: Was it a.m. or p.m.? Went in the morning, street deserted but for man who opened his overcoat to expose himself naked to her. She bashfully looked aside, saw two rats copulating in the gutter. Query: Do rats under observation couple in broad daylight? Are there dental surgeries in Westland Row?

5 October
Ned Ward visited Dervorgilla in hospital. Injection delayed, in much pain, stoical, brave.

7 October
Aerogramme from James: 'Jane met us with a deep tan. England seems unusually dull and pseudo after Spain. *Yo busco trabajo*. Carlos singing out of tune as usual.' Died this week in Deya on the island of Majorca that vain poet Robert Graves (1895–1985), sometime *amigo* of the Kerrigans, buried in Deya cemetery with hat and cape. Died too that acid man Geoffrey Grigson, poet.

Through D's binoculars saw what I took to be large deer stalking through far-off meadow; turns out to be a pair of cavorting horses.

A couple called Mudde or Sludde are visiting D. today. Ned came at 8.00 a.m. to collect her backbrace.

Ned Ward is thirty-six to Christina's twenty-two. Alec Stone left his wife to live with another woman: such behaviour is 'frowned upon hereabouts', says Ned. As I fancy his liaison with Tina is frowned upon.

The year 1985 remains bizarre through the autumn: we had 'summer' in the month of October and on the eve of Oiche Samhna they were still saving turf in the West of Ireland. The chances of getting a bank of turf, being footed in the last week of October, to dry before the November frosts must be slim. The odds did not inhibit some cutters in Mayo. In places the struggle was to get turf saved earlier from sodden banks. Others found that turf 'lumped up' on the roadside, ready for tractors to haul it home, was sodden from the rains of summer. The October sun was not a great deal of help for it was a 'dead' sun with no back-up of drying wind to help evaporation.

31 December

Died this year: Shiva Naipaul in London, Italo Calvino in Rome, Axel Springer in Berlin, Simone Signoret in Paris.

At Chepstow races in wet green Wales the favourite Powerless was nowhere, while a rank outsider with the unlikely name of Pigeon came romping home at long odds. So ends this peculiar year.

All yesterday the phone rang persistently.

Someone is watching; someone is listening. A glow of fires along the hills and Shandon bells ring in the new year.

Not much of an obituary for Böll in *Die Stern*. He came before Grass and the Swiss Frisch who had helped Grass to get published. What hope had a German writing in German just after the war ended when *Tin Drum* came out?

Böll was suffering from severe circulatory problems in the legs; on returning home to the Eifel Hills after visiting hospital he died just hours after arriving. Böll was sixty-seven. Fortieth anniversary of Los Alamos tests in New Mexico.

Died this year: Heinrich Böll, Calder author, aged sixty-seven at his home near Cologne. I recall the big dome of a forehead freckled like a thrush's egg, pale blue exophthalmic eyes staring from a clown's face; a walker in the hills. He had been correcting the proofs of *Gruppen Bild Mit Dame* (Women in Front of a River Landscape) just before he died. The Bölls had a summer cottage on Achill, had translated *The Third Policeman*.

Also passed away: Patricia Cockburn at her home in County Wexford. She understood the language of pygmies. And at her home in Galway Mairie Ni Scollig died; how many years ago had I heard 'Eileen a Rune' on an old cracked 78 r,p,m, in Porchester Terrace?

All dead now, all the sweet singers gone into the world of light.

Dervorgilla Doran's symbol is a three-pronged fork. Co-habiting requires the nicest readjustments; as in the days of sail, tidal and wind shifts, management of sails, the chops of the Channel on a dirty night.

No smoking permitted in the salon.

The cup I was using was her favourite and could I please use another? Could I lend a hand with the garbage that was putrefying?

A breeze stirring the young pines disturbs the restless spirit of the dead Cooney. The wind blows through the wood; at night, tucked up in bed, I hear the sea pounding away behind the brake of pines.

Dervorgilla intends to let out the mobile home for an undisclosed sum this coming summer. The drains have already been dug and connected up with the sewerage system of the bungalow. The asking rate for Ballymona Lodge in high summer: £175 per week.

PART IV:

The Tomb of Dreams

The other day I came upon a diary I kept in 1977. That year I was the happy recipient of $7,000 from the American Irish Fund disembursed in some style at Arus an Uachtaran by the late William Shannon, the former American Ambassador, bald as a coot. It was a most timely subvention.

With Paddy Gallagher, the RTE cultural linchpin, as outrider and bellringer I set out to scour the west in search of suitable accommodation. This is the Dublin part of that diary, the summer of 1977 in the time of the Provo killings.

44

The Trinity Professor

D ublin was infested with mice in the twelfth century. Dung-heaps, free-roaming swine, hog-styes, noxious stenches from the slaughter of cattle polluted the air in the thirteenth century.

In the mid-seventeenth century there were wolves in Wicklow. A public wolf-hunt was ordered in the ward of Castleknock, only six miles from Dublin.

There are thirty abattoirs in Dublin today. Slaughtering goes on at night and at weekends. In summer, in hot weather, two ladies in Rathmines keep their windows closed and avoid the garden humming with bluebottles.

The Trinity professor wears fishnet stockings, suspender belt and bustier, a Cupid's bow painted on the lips with the reddest lipstick and hair tied back with a scarf. He-she likes to mingle with the Ballyfermot rough trade drinking tea in the kitchen of the whorehouse and they have been told to call him 'Mary' and not to laugh at her in her fishnet stockings.

When he-she isn't mingling with the hard men in the kitchen she-he has to do housework, and the whore is strict. The house can never be clean enough with this sloven Mary sighing and scrubbing the toilet bowl with her bare hands, thinking of the hard men in the kitchen. But it won't do, it's not clean enough, not half clean enough for the mistress, who has no choice but to whip the arse off this slutty maid, the dirty thing.

The Trinity professor has not had a natural erection since he was systematically beaten as a boy by the Brothers who made him what he is, the sloven Mary in the whorehouse who crawls on hands and knees, in fishnet stockings and falsies, and cleans out the lavatory bowl with her bare hands, and is beaten by her angry mistress.

Never before such disparity between those who have and those who have not.

The Dublin pimp takes up his position. Hidden from sight in the deep hanging cupboard he unzips himself and applies his eye to the small peep-holes he has bored at eye level and holds his breath.

In the bedroom under observation his whore-wife performs fellatio and unnatural acts with her grunting clients, unaware that she is under observation. She earns £700 a week. The husband in the dark watches, sucks in his breath, stands stock still, as the exiled Emperor at Longwood House on St Helena spied on the English watch coming on and off duty.

On the window-ledge outside the back bedroom at Emor Street, the weighing-scales fidget in the breeze. All night they fidget in the breeze and by morning the little pans are half full of rainwater.

Then the traffic on the South Circular Road starts and the early jets come in, whereupon the neighbour's dog howls. The mother spanks her little daughter. The child weeps.

The hidden pimp neither drinks alcohol nor smokes, but treats himself to expensive clothes, runs a Citroën. When his whore-wife goes off the game he beats her, plugs up the peep-holes with cigarette filters.

Two lapsed Republicans were shot dead in Dublin, as a salutary lesson for the rest. Seamus Costelloe, Chairman of the Irish Republican Party, had absconded with party funds from a train robbery at Sallins. When John Lawlor, the Ballymore Eustace haulier, revealed the whereabouts of hidden arms dumps to the police he had signed his own death warrant.

'Call me Gus.'

'I'm Imelda.'

'My pleasure.'

The hidden prompter couldn't believe his eyes or ears, no longer recognised his own bedroom nor his own wife, Milly O'Callaghan that was; both bedroom and wife had undergone a subtle transformation, substantial sea-changes, become film set and star for a porno movie.

'This is our new bedroom. Fancy a drink or a snack? Are you peckish, Gus?'

'Ah, now, Melly . . .'

The sleazy dialogue is spot on, the bedroom transformed, the bedclothes turned back, the curtains drawn, the door locked, the TV pushed aside, the carpet Hoovered, obese client and whore-wife already buck naked. Gus is blowing out his cheeks like a bullfrog, unsober enough to act brave and bold, outspoken about his requirements, gazing down complacently upon his own particular hairy grossness.

He lies on the bed as though it were his own, his greasy head resting on the pillows, gazing down, a glass of Paddy balanced on his hairy chest; a heavy-breathing adenoidal type with unhealthy skin white as ebony, matted curly black hair, a regular forest darkening the armpits.

'If I said I wouldn't come in your mout', Melly, I'd be telling a lie. You know, like saying the cheque is in the post.'

The hidden husband is rigid as a hare in its secret form. What did *abasement* mean?

In the hanging-cupboard he can neither blow his nose nor clear his throat and can hardly blink his eyes, riveted to the peep-holes. Oddly enough here is another Fergus, unless he is sailing under false colours and using an assumed name.

'Ah now Melly.'

'Ah now Gus.'

Trousers about his knees, grasping a fistful of tissues and breathing shallowly, his eyes fixed on the action, the concealed pimp is tense and rigid as a hare confronted with a hound.

'Ah now Gus . . .'

'Blow me, Mel.'

How teasingly adroit she has become, his Milly, profes-
sionally tarted up, that is to say provocatively undressed to
velvet black choker about the neck, one snappy red garter
about the bulging thigh, false eyelashes, eyes heavily made up,
rouged nipples, the works, and all to pleasure this slug with
hands clasped behind his neck as if casually sunbathing on the
Sandycove sea wall. The pimp–husband whose name is Fergal
grasps himself and applies dilated pupils to the peep–holes,
preparing to ejaculate with the client who now is reduced to
uttering a series of great hollow sealion hootings as the
kneeling whore–wife, stilettos sharp as daggers, works upon
him. In the bedroom that seems to expand and contract he
utters a great hollow staglike bellow, a terrifying mating call,
and plunges both hands into her hair, fuzzed up, crimped and
dyed black.

In a trice the Cork train has departed from Platform 2, sucked
into the void. Imelda Lurcan will never be found.

'We Irish think thus,' *pace* Bishop Berkeley, the tar–water
expert. We think as we do because we do as we think; but
who do we think we are? My late philosophical friend Arland
Ussher phrased it elegantly: 'As our forefathers thought, we
act; and our descendants will act out what we thought.'

Tame perks everywhere in Ireland, dog agility courses, Ho
Chi Minh (He Who Illuminates) walks, Crazy Prices,
Chinese and Italian takeaways, dual carriageways to all points;
golf ranges, heritage and interpretative centres, safe houses
and Dawn Meats; perfect piggeries; a time–clock in every
oven and a big fat bun in every one. A jumbo–fridge for the
rich O'Hanrahans and jumbo–jet to foreign parts for the nice
Miss Kerrigans. (Client and whore–wife are buck naked as if
about to try a few falls at all–in wrestling or undergo a medical
examination; her fingers sink into his soft yielding flesh as into
plump blancmange. Obese and hairy Gus wears only black

socks, perhaps ashamed of hammer-toes or for some whimsy of his own, an act of pure bravado.)

The sudden shadow of a flock of wheeling pigeons crosses the patio of sunflowers, circles about Avoca Road and Orinoco Street, settles on the ridge of the roof of the City Building Suppliers opposite Mick's shop. The old lady scatters Marie biscuits in her cramped back yard fetid with their droppings. Two hundred and more of them line the roof above us, keeping an eye on the giving hand; you can smell them when the breeze blows in the wrong direction. The melancholy drone of bagpipes, like a giant sobbing, the blackbird singing *Aujourd' hui!*, the low shifting clouds; all tell you it's Dublin, shower or shine.

In Searson's snug opposite the humpbacked Portobello Bridge, behind coloured glass, tobacco fumes hang dense. Jack Yeats used to recuperate in the nursing home opposite, after an exhibition at the Waddington, and give the nurses hell. Now it's a region of saunas, massage parlours, whore-houses.

The antiquarian bookseller uses the snug as his office. He is on the phone to a client in Killiney. A thick bunch of keys depends from his waistcoat pocket. Now he replaces the receiver. Now the door closes behind him. A truculent young worker with lime-stains on his blue overalls is calling his mammy in a gruff, manly fashion:

'Hello, Mammy. I'm just after walken in this min-yute. Can you put on me dinner right now?'

45

Walking in the Dream

I t is the last day of a curious year.
   A grudging daylight already fading by three in the
afternoon, a frugal grudging daylight leaking away, just as
before, as I seem to recall from the days of my youth. It's this
melancholy climate that makes the Irish what they are:
Farsoonerites to a man.

The weather is neither good nor bad, an overcast grey day.
Typical Dublin weather, you might say. Sea-fog and river-
mist mixed; turning to fucking drizzle in the late afternoon.

Turned fifty this year.

Basho's age when, ill again (dysentery?), he undertook that
last marathon hike into Japan in 1694. A year younger than
Jane Bowles (be good enough to move on three centuries)
when she died of a heart attack in Malaga, Capital of Sorrow.
In a snail-bar in the brothel quarter I came upon the ghost of
Terry Butler (RIP) late of Shanganagh Bridge and Bologna
(and never shabby in life) who failed to recognise Rodrigo de
la Sierra darkened by long tramping in the Almijaras.

Tired of walking in the dream I have returned to the country
where I was born half a century ago; it doesn't feel like the
place I knew any more; it appears to be most dreamlike itself.
'In my dreams I wept,' Heine wrote.

Great greybacked herring-gulls squall over O'Connell

Bridge where thin itinerant children beg, as their mothers before them, as their mothers before them, theirs before them. So much for the waste and futility that is our world. The gulls release their heavy loads.

The Liffey hasn't changed much. Anna Livia smells as before, oilslick and Godknowswhat flow by the Corinthian Cinema, its neon red lozenges reflected in the river are Rimbaud's 'Arctic flowers that do not exist'. Sluggishly stinking she crawls on, dragging her effluent out into the bay. I am in Dublin again; everything tells me so.

The shabby buff-coloured city conveys the overall impression (a shrug of the shoulders) of 'Make the best you can of what you have, it's all there is, there's nothing more.' 'Feeling only so-so,' they used to sigh forty years ago; 'only fair to middling'. Reasonable health was very much an off-chance.

The environs abound with unpleasant innovations (piped Muzak in buses) as well as pleasing old familiarities: the illuminated Bovril sign over College Green has been taken down, but immortalised in Beckett's *More Pricks than Kicks*; Magill's remains in Johnson's Court.

Are the memories of things better than the things themselves?

The city has changed in my absence, you never know how these things will turn out. Within the airless precincts of the modern lounge in what was the Sign of the Zodiac is a man of double deed in grey suit and bow-tie, sitting on a high stool with drink in hand, smoking a cigar and immersed in *True Detective* ('I Tried to Make It Look Like Rape'). The lounge is ruthlessly modern in a chintzy way with metal scrollwork in curlicues, phallic beer-pulls with hunting motifs and Las-Vegas-type cash registers for ringing up the change.

Renaults, Cortinas and a Mercedes wait in the reserved parking lot of the Meath Hospital, with a surgeon's squash racquet thrown into the back seat of the Mercedes. The countrybred nurse shouts loud personal questions of an intimate nature, as though interrogating halfwits. Porters stand about in green smocks. A dead man is pushed in on a stretcher.

Wishing to be well, when not exactly ill. Wishing to be ill, when not exactly well, I want everything to be still and at the same time everything to be in constant motion. And I want both to happen at the same time. Can that be arranged? The cock always crows at one o'clock on the third day of March every year for me.

Nico's in the evening.

'Were you at the Curragh today?'

'I was.'

'Had any luck?'

'I had.'

Pause.

'Is Tom inside?'

'He is.'

Longer pause.

'Tell him Mickey wants Jewish macaroni. Macaroni from Jerusalem. Tell him that.'

Night approaches.

The bus crews are drinking quick pints in Agnew's of Anglesea Street near the quays. Spent cartridges in William Street gutters, shattered windscreen glass and clots of blood (presumably human) in Dawson Street opposite the Royal Automobile Association. The renovated Mansion House is like a Christmas cake with icing or a Christmas tree stiff with false hoar-frost; Yeats would have been pleased. No beauty but hath some strangeness in the prescription. The postmen and the garbage collectors are on strike.

The dead are all around; very dear friends all gone home. We cannot escape them, even if our memory retains only indistinct images of them. Death is a silent picture, a dream of the eye; such vanishing shapes as the mirage throws.

An old Pope died in the Vatican. The Pan-German, pre-Socratic thinker and proto-Nazi Martin Heidegger died in Messkirch, his home town, aged eighty-six years. He had been influenced by Parmenides, Heraclitus (flux) and

Hölderlin (insane); arguing that being (*Sein*) cannot be
thought but remains a question raised by thought. Farewell
the old fart.

Also passed away this year: Cearball O'Dalaigh, having
fallen off a ladder in Kerry, who resigned the Presidency on
an ethical point, and whom I once heard speaking the most
mellifluous Gaelic to issue from a man's mouth, dressed as for
a safari in bushboots, a sand-coloured outfit, officially opening
an alfresco sculpture exhibition by the Limerick sculptors in a
field near the sea. Do not come down the ladder, Cearball, I
have taken it away.

Also died: Dr Micheál MacLiammóir (born Alfred Will-
more of Cork) whom years before I had seen prancing like
Nijinsky's faun on the boards of the old Abbey stage,
preposterously got up as Aleel in a daringly brief white shift
short as decency would permit, in Yeats' no less preposterous
play *The Countess Cathleen* ('Did that play of mine send out
certain men the English shot?'). Thespian, playwright,
painter, linguist and man of many parts, he was one of the rare
sights of Dublin, passing through in heavy make-up, or
emerging from one of the Gents in Stephen's Green; an
emanation from a previous age, a dandy in war-paint, an
alarming fairy. Once I had seen himself and Jimmy O'Dea,
dressed as women and camping it up with eyelashes and pouts
at a great Christmas panto at the Gate.

The bagpipes played mournfully all through one miserably
wet afternoon in Emer Street near the South Circular Road
in the Liberties, the gasometer sinking, the gulls squalling.

I ride through Time. Dead times and places return to life,
the dead walk again. Two in particular, a man and a woman.
Peter Allt was killed stepping on to electrified railway tracks
somewhere in England, *en route* to academic tenure in
Holland. Gerda Schurmann (née Fromel) was drowned in the
Atlantic attempting to save her son Wensisclaus who had got
into difficulties in the water off a Mayo beach.

I see them walking around Dublin with set faces, seemingly
ashamed of themselves and as if under punishment, con-

demned in some way; averting their eyes they hurry by, never together, always alone. Had they met through me, when alive? *Defunctos* are everywhere. Whenever I pass, afoot or by bus, the new high-rise apartments in Abbey Road, Kilburn, London, I think of Gerard Dillon (RIP), who had lived in the basement of his mad sister's flat with a large gingery cat called Whiskey. He used sand in his paintings, worked as a night-porter in some West End gentlemen's club, toting baggage and stoking the boilers.

He moved to Dublin to begin his death, sharing a house with Arthur Armstrong, another Northern painter; and died of the third stroke that he had feared would finish him off, which it did, in his fifties, as two brothers before him.

Condemned, they hurry past with heads averted. Some of their *horror vacui* infects me. But then horror is perfectly natural. Our history is not as others know it. Never was; never will be.

On reclaimed ground at Ringsend near the site of another Provo 'execution' (in Irishtown Seamus Costelloe got it in the face with a double-barrel shotgun) the soccer players are struggling.

'Hurra, chaps, for the man who got the curly goal!'

'Clap for the north wind!'

In Grogan's of Castle Street an inebriated man shouts in mock-rage 'Fasschist baste!' A couple of hopeless cases sit boozily on the steps of a deserted house in Liberty Row, staring at their broken boots. The silver beech saplings dance alongside the canal near Paddy Gallagher's dream-house. He too gone to his reward.

Permanently worried and permanently watering pale blue eyes follow the close print (at Shelbourne Park dog track the brindle bitch Glen Rock 'literally staggered' from the No. 2 box and failed to reach the first bend; urine tests had been taken; at White City in the English Derby, Glen Rock hit the rails).

Customers come in for loaves of Boland's bread and bottles of Lucan Dairy and Mick serves them absently, lost in the

dream where Glen Rock is hitting the rails at White City or
coming drugged from the No. 2 box. His big redfaced son is
in the Gardai. His shop smells like a country shop in the
country of my childhood (King's in Celbridge) when everything alarmed me.

Mick looks dead-beat. He lights up a fag, covers his puffy
face with a soft stubby hand, the index finger darkly stained.
MAN HELD FOR PUB MURDER declares the *Evening Press*
headline. The Ballymore Eustace haulier John Lawlor had
been shot dead by the Provos in Timmon's public house in
Essex Street one lunchtime: summoned there by the hit-man
ordered to 'execute' him and shot with as little compunction
as the killer would have given a mad dog; Lawlor sipping the
coldest pint he was ever to swallow.

Mick heaves a heavy sigh, licks his fingers, turns a page.
Skies over Dublin, shower or shine; the subsiding gasometer,
the ebbing Tolka, the filthy incoming tide dragging the weeds
this way and that; skeletons of bikes thrown in, sodden bread,
squalling gulls. So, so, it must be. *Es muss sein.*

46

Native Son

O ne grey morning in Timmon's didn't I fall into conversation with a garrulous returned Native Son who had lived for many years in a poor part of New York and was now back in Dublin where he had found employment in St Brendan's, formerly Grangegorman Lunatic Asylum.

In his high apartment he had paid sweeteners – bribes or protection money – to the Costa Rican garbage collectors. Otherwise your garbage wouldn't get collected, or they'd do something unpleasant with it. Speaking of garbage, he had thrown Tennessee Williams out of his place one night; Williams was very drunk, had come with one of his bumboys. He thought that Brendan Behan was a shy man. I could have told him otherwise.

On another night he had to throw out an even drunker Burl Ives. He had seen Cassius Clay (Muhammad Ali to be) in the ring fighting Spinks. 'Clay took a punch from Spinks in the solar plexus that could be heard in Pittsburgh.' The story is repeated later, Pittsburgh becoming Phibsborough. He tells stories of suicides in St Brendan's, all true, 'as sure as you're putting that cigarette in your mouth'.

He feared for the world, the state it was in; a third world war would not happen; instead we would have world famine. Ireland had forgotten too soon.

Fifty per cent of the Dublin phone booths have been van-
dalised and all the phone directories stolen for lavatory paper,
the booths converted into urinals. Mick is out of briquettes.
Six bullocks are being driven by two herdsmen in dungy
wellingtons, what the Germans call *Blücher*, into the abattoir
in Swan Alley, for it's slaughtering time again. One of the
herdsmen in a crushed hat, seen from the back, is a dead
ringer for my friend Paddy Collins.

A young bloodstained burglar was caught red-handed at
three in the morning attempting to jemmy his way into
Rosita's sea-green Morris Minor. She had thrown on a shirt
and run out, armed with a bicycle pump, snatched up. The
robber had a screw-driver in his hand and explained that he
had been chased by a gang from Kelly's Corner. He was
looking for the Meath Hospital. 'Well this isn't the fukken
Meath Hospital; this is me fukken car,' said the Contessa in a
great wax.

The bloodstained burglar was most apologetic and staggered off into the night.

On a television mast at least twenty metres tall a lone blackbird sings over Emor Street, above the home of the RTE
producer Harris just returned from a short winter break in
Benidorm. A deranged boy is breaking up the crazy-paving
newly laid in his narrow back garden.

The Libyan wives are leaving Emor Street, baffled by the
English spoken by the Irish, by Dubliners in particular, which
to their ears sounds like some extinct foreign language. The
computer-expert husbands will follow in a month with the
Peugeots.

The student from Honduras is studying a book on
venomous snakes in an effort to improve his English. A fellow
over the wall three houses away practises scales on the bagpipes all through one long wet summer afternoon.

All the municipal dumps are closed; the nearest one in
operation is out at Lusk. The number of tourists visiting the
Republic is up by 14.5 per cent, revenue up 32 per cent.

Two-thirds of the rainfall normal for the month of August fell in the inner city alone; in several places there was thunder and lightning.

Eight inches of mud engulfed the Scout jamboree in Woodstock, Co. Kilkenny. Despite the mud and overnight rain the 4,000 parents and friends who visited the camp found the 2,000 Cub Scouts in good spirits and the Camp Chief danced with the Girl Guides from Vienna. French Scouts cooked crêpe Suzette, Ringsend Scouts dispensed cockles and mussels and some Dutch Girl Guides danced in clogs in the mud.

The the sun came out to provide a beautiful setting for an open-air Mass celebrated by Dr Birch of Ossory. Elsewhere archaeologists and patriots joined in a search for the grave of bold Robert Emmet.

A discoloured sun sinks behind the brewery chimney. Leaning across the narrow deal counter, Mick the chain-smoker studies the racing form in the *Evening Herald*. Sunk in thought, the blue eyes water, following the print, the last third of a damp fag glued to a pendulous wet underlip. The puffy features are unhealthy, the body bloated like a toad, smoke gets in his eyes. Old Puffy Face, look forth! Not that Mick is old. He must be about my age, but he looks bad, a swollen caushapooka suppurating in damp aftergrass. Mick squints at the form sheet, his fingers stained to the joint by tobacco as if dipped in cowshit.

All's well in the Liberties!

47

Down in the Country

It was the worst winter in living memory, the coldest and wettest in Connemara since 1840. We, the Contessa Rosita and Rory, arrived in Bealadangan in October to take up residence in a modernised cottage rented out by Johnny O'Toole for six months' letting. It rained non-stop for the first six weeks and we feared that the thatch would rot. The old postman cycled over the causeway and arrived swathed in oilskins like Skipper, rain or snot depending from the wings of his discoloured nose. It was impossible to keep the turf dry; snow and hail came after the rain, icy draughts poured under the door or blew down the chimney to put out the fire.

At night in the attic the rats cavorted, making no attempt to modify their antics or go about their nocturnal affairs silently as you would expect normal rats to behave.

In the cold winter kitchen we found claw prints on the dried grease of the frying pan. In the chill bathroom, rats' teeth- and claw-marks on the Pears soap. At night we heard them running rat races in the attic, enjoying rat hoolies in the deserted kitchen, come drunk from the skips of the pub opposite. An Hooker was a haunt of hostile Gaelic speakers in knitted woollen caps who shot pool: 'spots' and 'stripes' were their only English words. A few of them spoke English, but most reluctantly; the sad bachelor on an old and venerable

bicycle who could name all the pubs on either side of Kilburn
High Street. Sean Claherty the carpenter had returned after
eight years working in San Francisco.

The late-arriving Gaels were known as Milesians in the
Book of Invasions. The first Mesolithic Man reached Ireland
at the beginning of the sixth millennium BC (6,000 BC) across
the narrow sea. Even at the end of the Mesolithic Period (*circa*
3,000 BC) there may have been only a few thousand inhabitants on the island. The laws were not committed to
writing until the seventh or eighth century, or thereabouts;
one cannot be more specific. The gap of 'world pain' was a
blank in Irish history; without Renaissance or Reformation,
let alone Auschwitz caesura; the Irish were nonparticipants
nonpareil with a hey-nonny-nonny no.

Out of the medieval darkness that stretched back into a
Gaelic infinity came the first public lighting to Dublin in 1689
to a population of around 40,000 souls; gas lighting followed
in 1825. But before that came the Norsemen out of the dark
sea with their battle-axes, helmets and devil's horns, great
hewers-off of simple Irish heads, great lusters after fresh Irish
maidenheads and pillagers of churches, despoilers and
desecrators of holy things.

The natives, ever adept at learning a hard lesson, repaid the
debt for dishonoured sisters and mothers with compound
interest, blinding and mutilating in their turn quite in the
rough and ready Norse manner. For oppression breeds crafti-
ness and hones the native cunning, breeds ultra-cruelty in its
turn; inbred cruelty the cruellest of all, the long-deliberated-
upon vengeance of the long oppressed. No greater oppressor
than those who have been long oppressed and woe betide
those who fall into their clutches.

While Belfast gets roasted by fire-bombs, Connemara is
drenched by Force Ten gales.

The old grievances take on a new reality here; Cromwell
mounted on a black stallion chases Pearse Ferriter on foot
through the bogs, dispatches him with a sword-thrust

through the fourth rib.

The cornerboys of Carraroe and Costello Cross no longer go to Mass but stand sullenly in the lee of the newsagent's shop, pawing the nude model-girl who smirks back at them in flaky colours from the front page of the *Sunday World*.

Granite boulders in which are embedded feldspar and pink potash are scattered about Costello Cross as if pitched there in the giants' battles of prehistory. They loved fighting amongst themselves down there then, bedad they did; first mythical battles, then real ones. Sufficient to say, the scroll of Irish history, with its quota of misery, blood and bluster, is still unfolding and unwinding.

I left Connemara and the weeping Contessa for a pueblo in the foothills of the Sierra Almijara in August; into the hottest Andalusian summer in living memory. In Malaga the thermometers registered 110 degrees and the birds dropped dead in their cages. No rain fell in months and the vines perished. The children took me for a Frenchman. In Connemara with my superior accent I had been taken for an Englishman and as such became the butt of Gaelic-speaking young pups disguised in their own language as in the folds of an enveloping cloak, muttering 'Up the Republic!' at the end of a chill bar in Carraroe, that sullen, misshapen village without a centre.

In the chilly pubs of Galway an obsession with maggots and worms prevails: the cheeky curate in the bar spoke of Herod's maggoty corpse and in the open vegetable market I encountered the double negative interrogative when a raw-faced woman tried to sell me a stone of potatoes.

'Ye wuddent be wanten a stone or tua spudds, I don't suppose woodja??'

One final word from the Gallows Bar, Galway.

Brisk dialling of taxi rank.

Punter (a Mr John Small): 'Hellew there . . . wouldja send a taxi to the Gallows please?'

Taxi rank: 'Where?'

Punter (patiently): 'The Gallows.'

Taxi rank: 'Where?'
Punter (resigned): 'The Gallows.'
Taxi rank: 'What's the name?'
Punter: 'Small.'
Taxi rank: 'Right you be, Mr Small. I'll be right there.'
And he was as good as his word. It was pouring with rain on Eyre Square as usual.

Ireland is the most westerly country in Europe. It is twice the size of Switzerland but not itself a part of Europe, geographically or in any other way; one more step and it would have been into the Atlantic. It's as far out as the wind that dried your first shirt.

Of the four fertile provinces of Ireland, Connaught is the least fertile but the most westerly; and Connemara the most westerly part of Connaught. As is well known, the Protector (no protector of things Irish) tried to confine the entire Irish race therein, like pigs in a poke. He thought he was dealing with aboriginals, heathens, and acted accordingly.

Ireland is in many respects a melancholy place. Melancholy is the projection of a psychic state; in this case brought on by the centuries of occupation, a fixed subjugation. The sun is low there in winter, the days are short and weak daylight fades away in the afternoon, the nights long and black as a skillet. Day breaks reluctantly again, the low clouds dripping rain; high water and floods everywhere, swamped fields, the snow melting slowly off the Maumturks, the bars closed, the cornerboys clustering in the lees of walls, the toilets overflowing. A sheepdog trots by on the road, watched by the marble eyes of drenched sheep high up on the slopes of the mountainside. Seaweed drying on the fretwork walls, a *pucán* rotting in the harbour, the moon down behind the Maumturks, the wind getting up at four in the morning, the sycamores trembling.

There are signs (someone laid out the seaweed) and sounds (a donkey-engine meliorating out in the bay) of human habitation, of the humans themselves there is no visible sight.

Is this the essential charm of the West, under the flying clouds? Its emptiness. The skies over Mayo would make you dizzy.

The whole country is flooded. The lock is in the door. The bog is wet. Con is growing. The place is cold but wholesome. Never leave your country. God is generous. Con is blind. Una is young. A man can't be in two places at once, unless he's a bird.

'There is no beauty but hath some strangeness in the pre-scription,' wrote Lord Byron with his quill pen; and he is a lord, a man who knew whereof he spake. Strangeness. A hundred square miles of island-studded water, haunt of mallard and widgeon, ptarmigan and cormorant, moorhen and gulls, swans upended in tarns of lapis-lazuli. The strange-ness of the known.

The gently rolling hills of Iar Connaught where romantic scenery abounds around every corner! Eyes of a bullfrog straining, veins in the forehead swelling, ceili music and set dancing, guided walks ('Corkery's Hills'), tame perks and much tomfoolery, learned lectures ('Corkery's Water-colours'), the twittery beat of the banjo, 'The Rose of Tralee' sung at closing time. And then?

'They do live on maggots.'

'Cockroaches an' lizards an' . . . schnails.'
    'Whassaaa – *schnails* is it?'
    'A small little fella altogether.'
    '*Scchhnaills?*'
    'Slugs is all right.'

'I'll not take anudder wan . . . oh God no.'
    'A fine big duck now . . .'
    'Turkeys' eggs . . .'
    'Ho–ho! the bluddy buggers!'
    'Starten to lay now . . .'

'Dark it will be until dis night is out.'

'Turnen out bad . . .'

'Getten very windy.'

'That was the time you'd fly home by nine o'clock.'

'An' still they were happy. There was nature in the people den.'

'*Scchhhnaills*, is it?'

'Are ye goin?'

'I yam.'

PART V

Ballymona Lodge, 1986

48

Brittas Bay

Weak January daylight cannot harm the fragility of the Turner watercolours on display for one month in the National Gallery by the terms of the Henry Vaughan Bequest. By pure chance I walked into the room of Turners years ago. In an adjacent room the entire *Liber Studiorum*.

Constable observed Turner on varnishing day at the Royal Academy: 'Turner has been here and fired a gun.' It was his second visit. He studied his canvas – 'a grey sort of affair'. After staring fixedly at it for some time he added a dab of red and instantly a red lead circle converted itself into a mooring float. Turner cleaned and wrapped up his brushes and went home.

John Constable had a sick wife ('I do not contemplate a happy old age') and has been painting the same subject for fifteen years; a state occasion to mark the opening of a bridge over the Thames. Homage to that peerless recorder of that day on the river; a crowded barge, flags flying, clouds scudding, hats waved, a festive occasion, huzza, huzza! How many times had I passed by Constable's house in Well Walk, Hampstead, coming to and from the Heath? 'Beauty lies in the eye of the beholder,' my mother used to say. 'Good bones will tell; breeding will out.' She was a great snob and fancied Anthony Eden in his homburg hat and pinstripe suiting. The Suez fiasco finished him.

Fine buildings, bridges and piers retain their dignity even as ruins and can improve with age; whereas advancing years do us humans no favours. What woman, an acknowledged beauty in her prime, can hope to keep her looks as an octogenarian weak in the pins, with false teeth, going deaf, the gloss gone from the skin as the sheen from the hair? Let alone as chapfallen crone of ninety winters, deaf as a post, balding, memory going, mind in ruins, a sorry spectacle wrinkled, grey and foolish. The raging beauties strip down to skeletons; they are no longer recognisable as the persons they were before, the cruel years having worked upon them, done irreparable damage.

Baroness Blixen eaten away by tertiary syphilis, a wedding present from Hemingway's gun-bearer, Blore Blixen. Djuna Barnes with her multiple ailments, aged ninety in Patchen Place. Louise Brooks aged ninety. Gloria Swanson, an old hag.

More snow on the back ranges of the hills lit by weak mid-morning sun, presently vanishing into the mist. Pork fillet unfrozen and now under fan oven heat; bottle of Spanish plonk chilling in fridge. Cash Murphy and dishevelled friend padded by on foot, up to no good I'll be bound. Overcast all day; miserable aspect without cheered by crackling of wood fire. Hard dry oak and yew are rejects from Ned Ward's hurley stick factory, brought by Ned in his wheelbarrow. He also brings me gifts of lamb chops which I cannot eat, and river-trout in season, small and quite flavourless. His father was a great hunter and trapper who kept the Ward family going during the war, in Roscommon.

Wednesday, 8 January
Weather cleared and weak sun shone by one o'clock, barometer steady at 45 degrees, cold persisting. More snow fell on back ranges of hills during the night. Twenty or more cars passed the gate heading in the Wicklow town direction; a funeral, but whose? Sodden rowan leaves and windfalls rotting on gravelled driveway. Depressed by bank statement

that shows £3,000 reduced to £1,500 within two months. In pitch darkness I hear firm footsteps passing by on the road. Who? Slept ill. Difficult to rise.

Nine years before I knew him Ned Ward had the near-fatal accident on the Loughlinstown Road. He was driving his wife and baby Nelly back from the nursing home when a Jaguar travelling at high speed went out of control and ploughed into them. Ned was crippled for life, baby Nelly thrown free. The other driver was killed; no relatives of his called on the injured couple in hospital.

Ned Ward and friend out shooting pheasants or rabbits. His girl rents a flat above Ann Lait's office for £20 a week. It's unheated but not cold, a bargain at the price. Ned's brain-damaged wife has been in hospital under observation these ten years, reduced to the mental age of ten. She has become child-like.

The wife's relations disapprove of Ned and Christina cohabiting. He can lure young foxes out of hiding, breeds gun-dogs, is mad about hurling and, I dare say, Christina, and visits his wife regularly.

'Spread out, Glenealy – you're all bunched up!' howls a supporter at the hurling.

Re-reading Yeats' *Autobiographies*, an almost merry book, as Ussher thought *Ulysses*. Yeats himself compared the opening chapters to that of a playful tiger. One suspects that the sober Senator did not get much beyond the opening.

I saw Shelagh Richards taking a bow as the producer of *The Playboy of the Western World* at the Gaiety with Siobhan McKenna as Pegeen to Cusack's Christy Mahon.

Shelagh Richards's Sandycove bungalow was up for rent; I had phoned from Santa Cruz to Patricia Collins who told me that it was too late, Shelagh Richards was ill and probably dying, I should try elsewhere.

Today in St. Anne's Church in Dawson Street a Requiem Mass was celebrated for the repose of the soul of Shelagh Richards, the original 'Nora' in *The Plough and the Stars*, the last of the last.

She was married in the same church to the playwright Denis Johnston, and may even have been christened there. A son and grandson carried the coffin.

Her closest friend Siobhan McKenna read I Corinthians, 13, Though I speak with the tongues of men and angels. Des Cave of the Abbey sang 'Nora', many wept. Hugh Hunt flew in from Wales. Among the distinguished mourners were the painter Patrick Scott and Ulick O'Connor in a snapbrim velour hat. The committal was held at Glasnevin Crematorium.   *Irish Times*

Early March

Up bright and early, showered and breakfasted, offer of lift ('throw on your coat') to village by Biddy. Her son Laurence aged six has lost appetite, has a dry cough and spots (pink) behind ears. Dervorgilla consults Dr Spock and says it's measles.

Getting into her car Biddy informs me that vandals went on the rampage in Arklow the previous night and smashed windows; we should be prepared for them tonight. She had found a large black spider in the bath. A very bad omen.

Biddy calls on a friend whose baby (one of twins) died still-born; to find out the time of the funeral today. Then she decides not to go, because of Laurence and the danger of contagion. She drops me at the post office at 9.30 a.m.

I post a letter to Anthony Kerrigan in Palma. What's the Spanish for 'retained semen turns to poison'? *por favor*. Bought grey two-tone reefer jacket in Connolly's haberdashery for £28. The bright lad who serves me says jauntily that he is 'headin' off for the Big Apple' soon; jobs were there for the asking. No work permit needed? Not to worry, it can be arranged. Irish Mafia.

As I stand before the long mirror in my two-tone reefer with many pleats and side pockets, the child's funeral cortège passes slowly behind the hearse carrying the small coffin and the townspeople bless themselves and remove their hats. I am told that the little twin sister is just surviving.

The people of Wicklow town have a great fondness for funerals. In winter hardly a week goes by without a cortège passing through to the cemetery, with pedestrians stopping in their tracks, doffing hats, shedding tears.

With his backside to the courthouse and the mangy Provo bar the pikeman stands aloft on his stone pedestal, caught in mid-stride like Paavo Nurmi, brandishing a non-existent pike, stolen by late-night revellers from the Periwinkle Bar.

49

To Arms! To Arms!

Remote villages along the Connemara coast are rough as their own rocks, or a Red Indian reservation near Spokane during a Republican convention.

Hereabouts the youth are ever in a chronic state of flux and all on fire with poteen and Republican frustrations, thwarted ambitions and hopes mixed up with sour disgruntlement with their own unhappy lot; which is passing strange, seeing they are taking home wages hitherto undreamed of in their wildest dreams, the pay packets from Japanese fish-canning factories and the sea-farming of mussel and oyster beds.

In boulder-strewn Drim in the far extremity of the western seaboard the solitary pub remains open until two in the morning and mighty is the imbibing there where none dare leave sober, where few even *arrive* sober.

Ancestral anti-English prejudice thickens the air even further. It's a form of perverted patriotism, like running a car on gas instead of petrol, as happened during our Emergency (quaint Irish euphemism for World War II, which apparently was none of Ireland's business).

The cowboys or apprentice Provos see themselves as a daring combination of vigilantes and Community Alert, with the menace of hardline Ku-Klux-Klan, dangerous in their cups; i.e., most of the time. They do not like to hear the sound of the English language.

Hotheads such as these, seething with ancestral wrongs, real or imaginary, against all things English for ever and for ever, would have no compunction at all in obeying orders to shoot Captain Nairac out of hand or butcher the luckless racehorse Shergar, both perhaps buried at night, subsumed back into the Irish soil. (The land itself, never a spent force, is in its turn the instrument of a remote past.)

I have seen their opposite numbers in Derry and shuddered. As savages of the jungle paint their faces for tribal celebrations, or football supporters daub theirs with the colours of their teams, shake rattles and howl abuse indiscriminately at rival supporters and referee, so the Orange enclave of what used to be called Ulster, in a similarly provocative fashion paint their gateposts, gable ends and even the pavement coping-stones of the streets with the colours of the Union Jack. When a Protestant Unionist salutes the flag he salutes more than his own glorious past; he salutes his great good fortune to be born a Protestant in Ulster, salutes the Boyne victory and his God-given and granted tenure on the land, salutes himself as the potent reincarnation of all this grace and goodness.

Thus envenomed sectarianism is incorporated into the rich fancies, the heated faces, the faciae of buildings and for all I know the very faeces of these embattled bigots, these rampant Orangemen to whom the green white and gold is as a red rag to a bull.

Swift claimed that he could tell a Whig stool from a Tory's; but the men of destiny (obstinate as nippers resisting potty-training) incarcerated in high security prisons and held on serious criminal charges not excluding murder, would deny all; deny even the Court's legitimacy and right to try them in the first place, abrogating to themselves the God-given right to make a mess where and whenever they choose, and proceeded to smear the cell walls with their own excrement, hot and steaming.

It is a miracle, we may suppose,
No nastyness offend the skillful nose;
Which from all taint, with peculiar art,
Extract savor and essence from a fart.

To us Irish the figures of the past, our ancestry, have the reality of fixed destinies; with historical themes our dialogue is formed by our awareness of them as *fated beings*, invisible but alert and out there somewhere, the calamitous Catholic defunct (the faithful who by definition need no conversion).

'A people lost in the Middle Ages refound and returned to Europe. A free Ireland, a world nation after centuries of slavery' was how the patriot Sir Roger Casement phrased it, sailing for Ireland with arms for the uprising in a German U-boat loaded down with sanitary pipes.

In the frozen forecourt of the Hotel of the Isles in deepest Connemara in the depths of a freezing winter, the solitary palm tree shivers. In the poor empty bar a frugal coal fire dies miserably in the grate.

In a warm conservatory at Kinvara, Garry Nally sits snug. In the tidy living room of his neat Georgian house there squats a curious love-seat painted powder-blue, cornflower blue; it's Lady Augusta Gregory's bathrub with one side removed and some cushions thrown down for the lovers. We the pseudo-lovers, the Contessa Rosita and Rory, sit there and drink Jameson poured by a liberal hand. An aged Pomeranian wheezes on the thick carpet at our feet. On leaving, we are given bunches of grapes from the conservatory; it's real old-style Irish hospitality, the dram of whiskey, the kiss on the back of the hand, may the road rise with ye. We depart from Kinvara in good fettle.

One pale washed-out late November day in the Maum valley beyond Screeb I saw the white forms of distant sheep grazing on the steep slopes of the mountainside, reduced now to the size of lice.

A fierce dog the colour of a grizzly bear tore open a plastic garbage bag on the boreen to the beach. A single yellow court-shoe lay on its side on the sea road to Carraroe.

An injured St Bernard dog limps about the hall of Hyland's Hotel, its back broken by cruel boys. An aged sheepdog sleeps in the backyard. We drink in the deserted bar after midnight; the trusting owner says to leave tabs, pay when we leave.

The howling dogs of Castleconnell give collective tongue when the aged bellringer hauls on the rope and the church bell tolls the hour. Has this been going on for centuries? The dogs start getting uneasy five minutes before the hour and assemble in the middle of the road; they begin to howl as the bellringer hauls down the rope for the first loud clang of the bell. They howl loud and long, a most mournful sound.

An infatuated couple are glued together in an endless kiss near a wet wall in pelting rain on the drenched outskirts of Kilkenny town. Scores of hooks are screwed into the ceiling of a pub in Rearcross from which gumboots hang, as I speak to dowser and mystic Jim Armshaw who asks me my personal opinion of the Astral Body. The name Rearcross means nothing, it was a marking error on the Ordnance Survey Map, a cross to indicate a hamlet. Up to 1820 there were no roads; to 1887 no church, which was shipped from Scotland. The old IRA burnt down the barracks.

A winter butterfly emerges trembling from the woodwork of the bed we have dismantled, sluggish as a moth, all aquiver in the weak sunlight that penetrates into the chill bedrom.

A rainbow arches itself over the boggy land on an extra-ordinarily still November morning with the snowcapped Maumturks reflected upside down in the estuary. Someone is hammering on a roof, the sound meliorating off miles away into the still valley where the sober bachelor comes wobbling on his venerable bike, affecting to be pissed. Then a bout of brisk sawing; then absolute silence but for the distant cries of curlews, the air dense and quivering with cold.

Now the Maumturks are reflected inverted into the blue estuary where Johnny O'Toole (RIP) thirty years ago saw fifty hookers with sails set entering the little lagoon beyond the bridge where today two seals hunt mackerel, the bull

driving the shoal to where the cow waits, hidden, pretending
to be seaweed or a dark hole.

Their speed is astonishing in the water as they fire themselves at the shoal that scatters, frantic to escape those deadly
snapping jaws.

The two seals go hunting for mackerel below the bridge
where we watch; as the tide begins to flood in again. The
wind cuts through the struts of the bridge with a vibraphone
effect; down in the silence of the bright inlet the two seals
hunt to kill with vibraphone effects.

The purple grape-coloured and violet glacial mountains are
reflected all atremble in the estuary now. Silence of the
cemetery where great age improves the headstones and the
Celtic crosses; mildew and weathering have reduced the
pomposity of the gravestones under which lie the last remains
of several octogenarian males of the region.

One morning we surprised a hare sunning herself behind a
boulder on the beach. The causeways and the little granite
docks were built as relief work in famine times when
Gorumna, Lettermore and Bealadangan were islets of the
estuary, when the fifty hookers sailed past. Who is it speaks of
the void eternally generative, of occurrence as part of an
infinite series? Nietzsche?

I recall the Lake of the Blind Trout, the hare on the beach,
the court-shoe on the road to Carraroe, the huge men in the
pubs and their barely hidden animosity.

You could throw a stone across the little lake, really a pond
fringed with bulrushes; we swam across it in the nip, sat on a
flat boulder warmed by the sun. The inlets and tarns turn
from cobalt to lapis lazuli as the sun moves behind clouds and
the wind rises and the colours darken and the last leaves flutter
from the copse of trees and the Maumturks huddle together
for the only possible, to materialise and vanish, uncannily
freakish, as if playing games with the observer.

Reality is concreteness rotating towards illusion, or vice
versa, arsyversy; illusion rotating towards concreteness. The
Irish were Picts before they were Celts, Picts covered in

feathers and crippled with strange superstitions but perhaps happy in their way. The world (the earthball rotating in space) is much older than we had supposed. The smaller the island the bigger the neurosis.

50

The Old Flame

Encountered whom do you suppose in a month of Sundays but the Old Flame resolutely crossing Butt Bridge to Tara Street station. Her car was parked in Dun Laoghaire to avoid the city traffic congestion; she offered to drive me home. Her lending library books were the new Graham Greene and Ben Kiely. She wore a summer frock and chattered, delighted to see me. The train was packed with bawling babes that made her testy; she said she was crippled with arthritis, in America she had to ask them to turn down the thermostat, in restaurants she froze.

Her car was parked by the yacht clubs. She drove like the wind, aged seventy-one years, past her old home in Dalkey where as a breezy young thing she had dived off the rocks and gone to school at Loretto Convent, never gave cheek to her teachers, was a dutiful daughter to aged parents, was a good girl long before she met me.

We flew by Dalkey Island where we went for a picnic one hot summer long ago, took photos of the goats slaughtered since, saw a condom on a boulder, were rowed back to Bullock Harbour. She was thirty-nine, I twenty-four; she said she was a baby-snatcher.

Punnets of early strawberries were for sale by the roadside, getting progressively cheaper all the way into Wicklow, famed for its strawberries as Aranjuez for its asparagus. Thirty years before we had eaten a punnet of strawberries in a field at Swords before visiting some relative put away in a mental home. We pulled in at a roadside fruit shop run by Spaniards; the mother was at the check-out, one daughter *hablar*-ing away in Spanish on the phone to Madrid, in a thoroughly Spanish ambience.

After Earl Grey, strawberries and cream, the Old Flame strolled in the garden and took cuttings, chattering away to herself. She used to say that when she talked a lot it meant she was happy. She was not an observant person, nor had much intuition about others, living alone, widowed, not greatly changed from the person I had known thirty years before.

51

The Far Horizon

Friend Kluger phoned from Berlin to say the city was very hot and humid. The boss of the Berlin Zoo was a great admirer of my novels.

He (Kluger) wants to come here late August for a trip West. Storms in Leitrim cause the River Bonet to burst its banks and sheep are swept away in floods at five in the morning. Grass of the uncut lawn beaten down by wind and rain, the rats in the outhouse digesting their poison. Mist and drizzle obscures the nearest hill, miles off on the far horizon.

The coal is damp, the wood won't burn, the rats are all poisoned, Dervorgilla away foreign. Only a Spanish station comes clear as a bell on the airwaves, male announcer going on about 'nueva perspectiva'; then some expert explaining the Aztecs in the language I love but cannot speak.

Mid-July drizzle of perpetual rain, awaiting arrival of orange mail-van seen speeding into Binnions's yard, with Blackie wagging his tail, preparatory to attacking postman. Pigeons cooing in Cooney's wood, wind rising, as I am handed the letter. A sweet missive from the Fruitcake, that variable lady born under the sign of Balance, the wonky scales, my ex-wife.

Front room: new rugs on floor, black lino paint around the edges, the books gleaming, inviting perusal, I hope, to those chaps.

Bornholm with Schocken. Favourable short review in *Publishers Weekly*.

Konrad's wedding in country. Maze of woods, marquee in clearing, garden full of summer people & summer children. A gracious figure came towards us with straw hat & gloves – mother of the groom – leading us straight to the marquee where none other than Kit Horner hoary & ancient stood. Looks as if you could blow him over. Overcome, watery-eyed at the sight of the three chaps . . . Soon there was wrestling on the lawn.

Very nice when most had left & the evening light slanted through the trees . . . Horner overstayed his welcome as usual, became incoherent. Rather frail figure, swaying across the lawn to have a piss in the trees.

I'm off to Boulogne this weekend with my boss Jackie Ennels. Back on Monday evening (4 days). Merry weather here with trees frisking about in the sun. A fond embrace.   J.

A small neat handwritten note on a cigarette (Old Holborn) roll-up gives an address near Barcelona:

> Valldoreix,
> Paseo del Romero 65.

Indicates the present whereabouts of Sean V. Golden, who gets about. In a briar patch in County Wexford some children out blackberrying found a leatherbound first edition of Carolan's harp airs. The *Cork Examiner* reports a 'spate' of moving statues of the Blessed Virgin, at Ballinspittle and in Kerry.

A Jewish jeweller comes down from Dublin for two months every summer to his bungalow near Ned Ward. They have lameness in common. The neighbour's foot was caught in a combine harvester and had to be amputated just below the knee. Ned refers to him as 'the jew-boy' without any malice aforethought; and this the same good Christian (Ned) who arranged for a pauper Dane who died penniless in Dun Laoghaire to be given a decent burial in Glenealy among Protestants in the Protestant cemetery. Sven the Dane used to drink in Healy's pub and Ned Ward made a collection there and got them out to attend his funeral. Was that not the act of a true Christian? Yet he can call his lame neighbour a 'jew-boy'; as he might call a Negro a nigger, or a spade a spade.

Cold morning shadows eerily slant from the side of the bungalow seen at an unusual hour, early for me, un-accustomed to warmed houses. Nescafé well laced with Jameson to hand.

Cycled to Wicklow by back road.

Arms of the harbour open to north-easter, pile of timber on quayside, little traffic going through, Healy pub closed induces a feeling of unreality peculiar to Wicklow port. The heart sinks.

Bought my vegetables from Fallon who used to sell stationery and typewriter ribbons. A box of greens for £5.50 and Anna singing as she makes out the bill, Michael (who formerly worked in a bank) whispering on the phone, organising contraband vodka. Crossed the bridge for gin and tonic at Leitrim Bar. Three fellows in black leather at snooker, Clifford Dowling (former butcher's boy) in one of his sullen moods. I hear fukken dis and fukken dat as I phone Sadie for a taxi.

Serene blue day with outside barometer registering over 60 degrees. Clumped out in heavy wellingtons across the Carmelite grounds by Stations of the Cross, no teasy novice lingering on rustic seat, no owl roosting above the path, no poachers gliding through; an old nun stares down from an upper window. A branch blown across the path by Hurricane Charley, a feeble game of tennis in progress on the hard court, deep rainwater pools on the path to the sea by the mucky farm, cattle bellowing in the byre.

I cross the meadow and over the dunes on to Magheramore beach to find the stream has changed course, now runs deeper and straight into the sea, too deep to wade across. I climb across the boulders on to Silver Strand. Sunbathers stuck into deckchairs outside summerhouses, transfixed in rigid poses of the sun-starved Irish longing for Benidorm. A little swell and collapse of waves on beach.

Scudding high clouds all day and sun going down behind distant hills in stupendous sunset, a mongrel sitting on kennel roof next door howling at it. Subside into armchair, push open sliding door: Hussar vodka and fresh orange juice on cubes of ice, what could be better. Rereading *The Periodic Table*, still mystified by the chemistry.

Biddy Doran has ambitions for her children, would have them talk nice, have nice manners. I hear them on the swing.

'Whin I ring the clock yiz must stop.'

'Now hold yer legs in or you might hurt dim.'

'Be nice an quiet.'

'Keep yer head down now an keep yer legs as well!'

'Goin roun an roun, dizzier an dizzier.'

'Ah GOD don't be holdin yer legs out!'

'Gimme a push. Give us a swing! Push me round about, fukken EEEeeejit!'

Dunganstown East, visit to Ye Moncken Holte.

Stella shows me the stiff yellowed pages of an album devoted to faded persons. Light thickens and the crows make wing to the rooky wood. My brother's fondest loves: Henry Williamson's *Chronicle of Ancient Sunlight* (in old Penguins) and the documentary films of Humphrey Jennings.

52

Stardust

'**W**ait here. I won't be long.'

Taking an empty petrol can from the boot my brother set off into the night.

An hour later he returned to Lil Doyle's to say he had had no luck; walked five miles in the Arklow direction and found no garage open. What he proposed to do now was to walk in the Dublin direction where there must surely be a garage open, even on Sunday night.

'I'll be back in a jiffy.'

Off with him again into the coal-black night.

An hour later the pub closed up and the lights went off. I sat on the wall outside, smoking roll-ups and looking at the stars. In a while my brother arrived carrying the empty petrol can: there were no garages open in Co. Wicklow on the Sabbath. My brother had driven over an hour before closing time and suggested a nightcap at Lil Doyle's. The Mini had run out of petrol just before the Barndarrig crossroads and we had coasted into the car park; where now we left the stalled car and set off on foot for Dunganstown.

Walking the back roads on the moonlit night my brother remarked on the movements of the moon, how she raced across the night sky in three hours, then vanished over the horizon. Where did she go to? What was she up to? He thought it was passing strange. And why so fast? And what about the Dark of the Moon?

'An assignation?'

My brother said again that he didn't understand Aristotle any more than he understood the movements of the moon. In previous centuries it was dangerous to travel on the roads; coaches were held up at pistol point and pedestrians set upon by footpads and cut-throats.

'Look at London in Dickens's day.'

He marvelled at the difficulty of obtaining fresh fish on an island (Ireland) surrounded by salt-water seas full of mackerel and fresh-water rivers full of salmon. He and his wife had been vegetarians ever since Stella had been put off meat by the stinks in a butcher's shop, from the days when pigs' carcasses hung on hooks and bled into the sawdust. They had enjoyed a very tasty herb omelette in Paris and decided then and there to become vegetarians, and had remained so ever since.

The moon went scudding behind trees into the clouds and then out the other side. My brother and I as lads had walked the front avenue at Springfield, puffing Craven A, passing along the road and up the front avenue past the lodge gate where the Keegans slept. We walked across Mangan's long field on stiff frosty grass and saw glinting moonlight reflected on the dormitory windows of the Collegiate School where forty or more Protestant orphan-girls slept, dreaming away the night. We now walked to Dunganstown heights where my brother brought out an antiquated rusty Raleigh to take me the five miles home, giving precise instructions how to get there. Having walked five miles from Barndarrig crossroads, my perambulating brother would have covered some twenty-four miles in all, without a drink. And without finding any petrol. The car remained all night in Lil Doyle's car park. Could he not have borrowed a pint or two of petrol to get him home?

Not him.

53

Lammas

Up at 8.00 to thunder and lightning, overcast and drizzle followed by downpour. A heron flying by, changing direction from hills to sea, outside barometer reading 60, down 10 degrees from yesterday.

Sunday Miscellany on RTE radio, a long-running arts programme old as the hills. Old-timer Big Ben Kiely, himself a reincarnation of Finn MacCool, the anecdotalist in the ingle, tells of a man aged forty who in his lifetime had lost forty-four overcoats. Ben himself will never see sixty again, drinks with the crypto-Fascists in the back bar of the Clarence Hotel on the quays with Brian Fallon of the *Irish Times* and the Austrian Ambassador; has a charge-account lunch preceded by a few drinks downstairs. After brandy and coffee and more tall tales, Ben noticed that his own new overcoat was missing from the coat-rack.

A brother is as easily forgotten as an umbrella (*pace* Mr James Joyce); but what about overcoats?

Telephone crackling as lightning strikes.

A grey crow on the fence-posts preening its feathers; line of silvery raindrops like mercury along the black handrail of drenched patio. Dread of the Chinese gentleman arriving from Kyoto, a Mr Steve Sakuma visiting Arklow 27 June to 6 July, with accommodation arranged. Letter from a Mr Steve Jusick of Indiana, USA, requesting a signed photo or a few

212

lines written by my hand from 'your great Scenes from a Receding Past'. Odd calligraphy. A Special Favor. An autographed collection of noted twentieth-century literary figures. Thank you for your very kind consideration. Your friend Steve Jusick 8212 Rutledge Mersill, Ind.

This occurred on Sunday, 29 June, being the third Sunday after Trinity, the Trinity term in the law sittings coming on to Lammas.

1 August (Lammas)

Appropriately enough a *slim* letter from publisher to say 'royalties are still being made up', a thumping lie I'll be bound, with a familiar ring to it. *Balcony* sales of 'nearly 3,000 at last accounting' from presumptuous first printing of 10,000 remaindered and sold off at cost price to collectors.

Invitation to sup at Sutton across Dublin Bay with Cantwells. Sunrise 5.25 a.m., poor class of a morning, hung around waiting for phone call that never came, set off on foot at midday, given a lift to Wicklow by English-sounding fellow in broken-down car, claiming to know Cash Murphy.

Walked from bar to bar, none too pleasing, then gin in Grand Hotel. Double of Anthony Burgess in wellington boots drinking Scotch and water. Took Wexford bus from outside hotel, sat on sunny side, boiling behind glass all the way to Bray. Made out £2.50 cheque to Dart, return to Sutton. Walked about Sutton looking for St Fintan's Road. Passed two Suttonites (male) out exercising two dogs (mongrels), then a single male pedestrian (dogless) who threw me a look askance, as if he knew me. He hesitated as he passed, then stopped.

'You wouldn't be Rory of the Hills by any chance?' said he.

'A piece of him,' said I. 'You wouldn't happen to know the whereabouts of Eamonn Cantwell? St Fintan's Road.'

'I do. I'm his brother.'

Dined on spaghetti and home-brewed wine, up talking until

2.00 a.m., slept like log in spare room. Rose betimes and crept out, not leaving note (impolite). At 6 a.m. snuck past Elmcot on La Vista Avenue in a cul-de-sac, the residence of novelist Banville, his back to the sea as Heaney's desk faced a wall. Six in the morning not the time to pay a surprise visit; let sleeping novelists lie.

Roamed about harbour deserted but for wandering dogs like myself. Took first Dart out to Connolly station. Harbour full of trawlers in from Friday's storm that sank a Spanish vessel. Sphinx-like enigmatic Oriental woman seated in stationary train, obviously a character from the novel Banville is writing. Doors whoosh shut, Tannoy stops announcing imminent departure, and the train leaves for Bray.

Bray station is like old times. A Greystones connection in three hours. Decide to hike over the Head.

Greystones has become a home for dogs, fouling pavements, assembling in packs, snapping at strangers. Dined alone in Magritte Room (*Tiens!*) at La Touche Hotel formerly the Grand Hotel in my parents' day, where Sam Beckett (probably in the bar) heard the news that the Nazis had invaded Poland and decided then and there to make his way back to Paris. Dined on half-bottle of Bordeaux and breast of chicken, small Magritte Room empty but for German couple near me. The loud confident male German guffaw that Beckett would have heard at the Closerie de Lilas at the close of day. Decided to overnight in Burnaby Hotel; retired early, stunned by air and hiking, slept the sleep of exhaustion.

54

James

Grand morning turns to gloomy afternoon with a wintry drizzle and cold rain blowing the birds about. While bathing my eyes there came a heavy thud against the front door. No challenge given, no word spoken, no loud abuse, and I with no weapon to hand but for Dervorgilla's trusty Turkish blunderbuss hanging on the wall. I waited for the door to burst open but nothing happened.

I waited, then drew back the safety locks and flung open the door to the light of a murky morn. No postal delivery van with engine running, no pale loiterer at the gate. I returned to bed with palpitating ticker and found with amazement the alarm clock in it. Who had put it there?

Almost dozed off when I was made to spring up again by a thud against the french windows. Took up heavy police torch, staggered into front room, found nobody there but a note in Dervorgilla's hand on the table which said 'Welcome home'. Flowers artfully arranged had already faded. Stale odour of unaired rooms after my few days' absence, signs of her careful occupancy. Know your neighbourhood; someone is watching. A heifer bellowing in the mist, fingers of rain scratching on the roof.

My son writes to me from London: 'For me the present is full of fear & uncertainty of what will happen to me. Salud para todos. Cuidate y escribame en tus ratos perdidos (spare time). Carino de su hijo James.'

I have invited him over for a week.

His old drinking buddy at the Baird, Alex Diggs (Scotch and splash) formerly of the International Brigade, has been cremated in Golders Green Cemetery. Why does he prefer friends either much older or much younger than he? They probably spoke Spanish together.

James is myself all over again, both troubled middle sons. The true misery began for him in Berlin, when I took up with Hannelore and the family began to split apart; classes in German after classes in Spanish. He attended the Nerja school in a white smock like the others, spent long hours in class, learnt nothing from Señor Pepito, a sort of Spanish Pickwick clapping his hands, ringing a bell, calling Jaime.

In Berlin, aged eight, he asked me: 'How did Jehovah ascend to Heaven in his bodily form?' Later he wrote of his *Mutti*: 'Her anger weakens me.'

Fathers don't see their sons. Not after the sons have grown up; the sons have begun to withdraw. I gave James 1,000 pesetas for his twenty-second birthday and he cashed it in a Torremolinos brothel.

Blind Hamm, the son, asks Nagg, the immobilised father: 'Scoundrel! Why did you engender me?' Nagg: 'I didn't know . . . That it'd be you.'

I don't see this thin middle son who stands six feet two inches in his bare feet, the whited extremities of an El Greco martyr, doing a Charles Atlas for the bathing girls of Brittas, gorging himself on Dervorgilla's raspberries and free-range chicken from the Belton farm; rather I see (a) a stocky confident child aged four standing on the upper bunk in a Ranelagh bedroom to recite something he had memorised for his granny, grandad and Uncle B; or (b) browned by the Spanish sun, aged six, the child who stood for hours by the stream behind Burriana to watch the water-bugs and frogs; or, hands clasped behind his back, the child who watched the palm trees being pollarded on the *paseo*.

His manner: slyly watchful, chastened and yet brash, uncertain yet persistent, contradictory, bilingually scatter-
brained. He makes me sad.

Aerogramme love-letters wing their way to all points of the
compass, for he is always in love, believing (wrongly) that in
a carnal Paradise full of geishas he will be liberated.

'What do you call it?'

'A cove.'

'An alcove?'

'No, a cove.'

'A cove can be a person too?'

'Yes.'

'How?'

'As a term of affection. They say "bloke" in London, here
it's "your man". A cove is a bloke, also an inlet, a little bay.
As this one.'

His light streams out from the mobile home, parked illegally
in the paddock, with an owl on the roof; he, being a great
reader in two languages, reads late. He is reading *Great
Expectations*, picked out from among Dervorgilla's few books.
The owl Minerva perched on the roof of the mobile home,
and another (or the same) on the telegraph wires humming
with gossip and hot scandal as we walked below on the first
night he came from his job as night security guard in a run-
down hotel or whorehouse on the Holloway Road. I noted
in my diary: 'I am six months here. 70 degrees by midday.
Many flies dart to and fro in the humid air, Blackie
kennelled.'

I recall the large puffy somnolent barn owl asleep on the
telegraph wires and the glitter of moonlight on the sea off
Brittas and the pleasure of having James with me, that I could
show him an owl asleep.

He naps on the sofa after I have fed him, complains that the
chops weren't brown enough, a little colour coming into his
face. Feed the starving. Free-range chicken, tinned salmon
and salad, tomatoes and onions, bacon, two brimming plates;

he does not eat enough in London or eats the wrong sort of food. He needs sleep, having outgrown his strength; the air here is soporific.

Supper of cheese omelette, bacon and rice, slices of ham. James in armchair, plimsolls removed, El Greco toes clenched, writing to Marina.

He has found some clip-joint in bashful Wicklow town and returns at three in the morning; I hear his plimsolls creep by on the gravel, and then his light goes out.

He says he loves Wicklow (already, quick to love) and prefers the Nuns' Beach to Burriana any day. I enquired how it had gone at the club. He drank water, was approached by a queer, 'heavy hints were made', he walked home. Hearty breakfast, toilet seat splashed with piss.

5 August

James departs, with country gifts for his mammy: dozen free-range eggs, jar of honey and apple pie from the Belton orchard, all good natural homegrown food for the family. James with glow in cheeks from walking, swimming, fresh air, changing punts for sterling, £20 plus £5 for the crossing. Sadness of his going.

For a week in July he was here with me, slept in the mobile home, walked the beaches, drank with me in the pubs, posed pectorally for the bathing girls, the lovely Brittas bathing girls, gorged himself in the raspberry bushes, lunched on mince curried in sherry, carrots and tomatoes, rice and raspberries and cream, reluctant to make eye contact (in case I should read his dirty thoughts?), retiring late to bed. 'Jane Austen has a habit of saying more than is necessary.'

Sun slanting through the young pines in Cooney's wood shines through the slats in the venetian blinds, reaches my table. September on the way and the days becoming perceptibly colder, though still preferable to the asphyxiating August heat of Texas – 'degrading', Eudora Welty called the New Orleans heat – those burning mornings when I left Palm

Springs Apartments for the campus and my two classes. Sickening heat on Guadalupe Street aquiver in the early morning haze. Fresh orange juice and natural yoghurt with coffee and croissants at Captain Quackenbush. Relax at Quax. Tar-black grackles croaking rustily in the thorn trees, the fountains dry.

Sunday, 10 August
A wren on the fence in the rain; inky clouds passing at sunset, a white breast-feather fell from the sky. All signs are omens, the cruel old Romans believed, auguries. A cunty smell of fish in the clean bathroom, both impossible. Could it be kipper grease or roes of herring? I am alone again. Dull throbbing pain in left eye. Anguished epistle from James who is in correspondence with José (*El Jardin de Allado*) Donosa.

> Dear Papa,
> I returned safely, a weary journey on the train. This is not love but a sort of sick, lost longing of desire. Marina moved into squat. I have changed too dramatically since I met her.
> I find I can only confide in you. You are my consolation, your presence. Will look for job, soon, soon as I get myself straight-ened out. I am weak, weakened from it all. Rory, tell me what to do, serious stern sensible advice is what I need.
> I don't love her. She can have an affair with Claudio who she's going to share the squat with. Dear Rory, mind your way & take care of yourself.
> Cuidate, J.J.

No sooner in the door than he began sending aerogrammes to Marina, whoever she may be; SOS signals, alarm flares, messages corked in bottles thrown into the sea. I too, at his age, was always besotted with someone, seeking salvation through love, itchy for response, any response.

James was ever a dreamer and a bit of a mystery, not least to himself, whatever about his estranged parents oft well-nigh demented with worry about him, the troubled middle son, which of course he played on as on a xylophone.

He was a baffling mixture of irreconcilable contradictions, charm and awkwardness, resourcefulness wedded to helplessness, forthrightness to furtiveness, flighty yet sagacious, simple yet devious. He read and spoke Spanish, drank Budweiser, was alert with a desperate *joie de vivre* – an inept boxer who keeps coming on for more punishment: night-guard duties in that dark building of ill repute on the grimy Holloway Road.

'Will you ever forget the time Uncle Dodo came down from Largs to visit us?'

'I won't,' said I; 'not to my dying day.'

The turdy old bollicks had come good at last; some years after his visit he had invited James to be his guest at Largs. A friendly fisherman had taken him out after mackerel in a rowing boat, and his silent uncle had cooked gigantic steaks for supper.

Henry Williamson, my brother's old favourite (his dog-eared and 'foxed' Penguins), was aged twenty-four when he published *Life in a Devon Village*, the same age as my middle son when he had visited Ballymona Lodge. Williamson had spent seven years in a Devon cottage with the barest necessities and two pet white owls for company when he wrote his Devon village saga and began assembling material for *Tarka the Otter*, which he would rewrite seventeen times. It was our favourite book, read to us many times by Mumu.

Williamson was a lover of nature, the great outdoors and its creatures; his favourite noun must have been 'estuary', his favourite place Ventian Sands in Devon. 'Every hour out of doors is an hour of immortal life,' he wrote; a sentiment with which my brother would concur.

During the war he ran a nudist camp in Devon, taking German female nudists, tall Fraus and Fräuleins, which did not endear him to the locals. As an old man he had visited Professor Burns at a house he had rented for a year in Battle main street and told him there was a three-week-dead shrew in the hedge. What a nose! I had come off an early train from London to Old Church House and Alan took me round the garden, told me of Williamson's wonderful nose.

It was the same Private Williamson who had crept close enough to the Boche lines to hear them talking, and flitted back to his own lines again, invisible as a poacher in the night.

'Every hour out of doors is an hour of immortal life'; Synge or David Thoreau could have written that, or John Clare.

I remember him standing on the upper tier of the bunk bed he shared with his brother in the garden flat at No. 47 Charleston Road in Dublin, reciting something he had learnt and memorised for his granny and grandpa and Uncle Bun and how he repeated all of it and would not be gainsaid because he thought he had had an indifferent hearing the first time. They all laughed at him but rather marvelling too, at his early sternness, a plump child on a bunk bed.

Or again behind Playa de Burriana staring for hours at a stretch into the irrigation stream at the Jesus bugs and the frogs.

Or again, with his hands clasped behind his back, studying the livestock in the yard of our apartment at Calle de los Angustias, a mule and a pig and fowl; studying them for hours as I came and went, unseen, on the balcony above.

In a very gloomy pub in north London (could it have been the Clissold Arms that was like the lounge of one of those liners sailing to India in the 1950s full of dull English people?) he had told me in great detail of a battle Cervantes had been in or had written about or had invented, he himself now long and lean as the Knight of the Rueful Countenance. Where had the plump child gone to?

Ezra Pound was ashamed of his parents when they visited him in London, ashamed of his daughter (whom he had abandoned and sent to foster-parents in Bavaria) when she visited him in Venice, perhaps even ashamed of himself in the traitor's cage in Pisa.

And I? I'm not ashamed of my son; wish him every happiness in his life. Sometimes he seems so *desolate*; he is myself over again, and yet not; it makes it harder for me to touch him. Why is that?

55

The Roscommon Fairies

I called on Ned Ward and found him working the power-mower. The carroty Joe Junior, one of seven redheaded brothers, was scuffling the gravel; it was the brother whom Ned trusted least and he liked to have him where he could see him. Christina was ironing clothes and the TV on full blast; the setter bitch and her straying pups were reunited in the wire cage by the gate.

I said I'd call back later and we might have a drink at Mac's.

John Stamp had piled up a fierce turf fire in the open hearth under the stuffed fox. Pint in hand, Ned was disposed to speak of his childhood in Roscommon. When the parents were out Aunty Peg looked after young Ned. One evening as he was preparing for bed a strange faery light flooded the bedroom. The Aunty blessed herself and said oh glory be to the God the fairies are moving house and you mustn't look at them. The Aunt would not let him go to the window to watch the fairies moving house. Lights were flickering along the path in the dark and the dog became hysterical and began barking and running round and round the house. The Aunt took out her beads and kissed the cross and told young Ned to say his prayers quick.

'A fairy breeze went by. I got back into bed. A fortnight later didn't a brother take bad and die in Birmingham.'

(Who was that Taffy poet who would not venture out at

night for fear of the fairies? His name escapes me. When he took to walking in the hills he felt himself to be *a different being*.)

The stuffed dog-fox in the inglenook had a melancholy glazed look in its eye as though it had suffered a painful death in a trap and been cut open, dosed with preserving liquids and fixed up with a pair of glass eyes lifeless as marble, then sewn up again by the incompetent taxidermist and wired upright on a wooden plinth. On long spindle legs it resembled one of the lean timber wolves that incessantly patrol their outdoor compound in the Dublin Zoo all winter long; as though by persevering a gap might be found in the high fence and the captive break out past the polar bears.

Ned Ward had lured a young fox out of a ditch by imitating a rabbit's death throes. He had come upon a dead stag in a ditch and sawed off its head, softened it up in a bath full of water until the stink almost drove him from the house. A friend was mounting the head and span of horns on mahogany; it would look well above Ned's trophies for marksmanship.

Ned drove us back to Ballymona Lodge; when his girl Christina retired and Ned joined me for a nightcap. I took out Dervorgilla's school atlas and showed him Mahón on the Island of Menorca and told him I would get there one day. Sand from the Sahara blew into the living rooms of high apartments.

Ned Ward and his two brothers were given huge meals of steak and spuds by a kindly Mrs Coffin in their Birmingham digs when they were working on the building sites from 8 a.m. to 8 p.m. He put in overtime, did extra work, bought himself a motorbike, ate huge meals served up piping hot by the kind Mrs Coffin. He put money away. At the end of the day he was knackered, dog tired.

He tells me this over a Chinese meal in Bray. In the headlights of his car we see a vixen fox trotting home, and a mile on, her cub, who gets confused by the light. Ned slows, the cub disappears into a weedy gripe.

Taking a drink in the Forge one day I heard a voice say 'the hay bogey', and later, 'in the haggard', and it occurred to me that soon these terms would be lost like Atlantis, words that had gone out of use, for things that no longer existed. Like the last Manx street-crier ringing a handbell, selling or buying junk, on a float drawn by a sad horse in Douglas on the Isle of Man. Extinct as the Manx language itself.

Pasture and paddock; were they the same?

'I cried all night,' a voice said. 'I cried my heart out.'

56

Big Mick (Ned's Racist Joke)

Big Mick of Cahirciveen was the tallest and strongest man on the building site but when he had the drink taken he would get out of hand and offer to fight the best man in the Eireann Go Brawl pub where they drank in Birmingham.

The lads got sick and tired of this and didn't they go and hire a gorilla from a circus, chain it up in the pub cellar and the next evening when big Mick got stroppy and started to throw his weight about didn't six of the lads lay hold of him, roaring and bawling, and fling him down the cellar steps, shouting out: 'Down with you now, Mick you big fucker and fight your match!'

Then a hurly-burly and almighty set-to began below in the dark (the lads having removed the electric bulb) with thudding uppercuts and piledrivers and deep gorilla grunts and hollow groans and the sounds of barrels and bottles fucked about and the stuffing being knocked out of somebody with thumping haymakers in the bread-basket, with blows landing loud and resonant as the big Lambeg drum being lambasted on an Orange parade that could be heard at Killybegs; then one final awful blow and dead silence.

The lads set down their pints and stared at each other. Gob, had the gorilla laid out big Mick? They were getting set to rush for the door when it blew open and there was big Mick in a lather of sweat, with the shirt torn off his back.

'That's the trouble with them black lads,' says he. 'Give them a fur coat and they start gettin' grand notions about themselves.'

The Afrikaans version of that joke goes something like this: unsober Afrikaner farmer is sitting drinking outside bar in Pamplona during the running of the bulls. He swallows his drink, spits on his hands and steps out into the street, takes hold of one almighty powerful Maura bull by the horns and throws it over on its back.

Amazing, said they; such valour, such strength, to throw a bull over on its back.

'A bull!' says the drunken Afrikaner. 'Is that what it was! Och min, I thought it was a bleddy Kaffir on a bike.'

57

The Screaming Horrors

On a voyage to Lisbon George Borrow saw a sailor fall from a crosstree in a sudden squall. A boat was launched but the men couldn't save him. They saw him below with arms outstretched and sinking ever deeper, and as he sank his life came up in streams of little bubbles. It is not an easy death, suffocation in salt water, but akin to swallowing glass. Borrow is the man who wrote about the screaming horrors.

It can be brought on by downing a plurality of pints followed by cold tea, which induces projectile vomiting. I have had the screaming horrors thrice myself, the last time in an old friend's house in Palmerston Park.

A female hand waved from the kitchen window and the little house-devil Scutty the dachshund began to bark, announcing my arrival. A sister was visiting with a grandchild and Granny was puffing black cigarettes and bullyragging her daughter who was thinning out baby food and testing it with the tip of her tongue. Then the Granny seized the infant's pudgy arms and went Guuuuggguuu! to distract the pet as the mother shovelled the food in and Scutty, naked as only a German sausage can be, spun around.

When they had all departed my genial host came beaming in with a primed tumbler of Paddy in either hand and behind him in the indigo glass of the conservatory I watched the darkness coming in the garden where we had unsoberly trimmed a bush until nothing remained of it but a stump.

Between the putting down of the glasses on the low table and reseating himself and resuming whatever subject he, the keen yachtsman, had been covering when he interrupted himself to fix the drinks, I had an unpleasant vision or visitation.

A company of six or seven Taoiseachs, the quick among the dead, sat stiffly upright in the conservatory which had broadened out and extended itself to twice and thrice its normal size to accommodate them. All were dressed in drab sagging snuff-coloured suits worn in the 1950s, Burton's off-the-peg that made them stiff as effigies in Madame Tussaud's. And there they sat silent and woodenly posed as for an official group photograph: Lemass, Lynch, Haughey, Fitzgerald, Costello and Cosgrave still as statues or lifeless figures in a waxworks.

There for a moment, silent and in sharpest focus; then they vanished, evaporated into thin air, and the indigo panes had perceptibly darkened and full night fallen on the garden, the garden had been wiped away and a distant voice was addressing me by name (Rory) and a hospitable hand held up a tumbler and for a blue moment of pure terror I didn't know who I was or where I sat; knew only the horror of non-entity, that which Proust recognised in the passing chambermaid's eye in the hotel at Combray or was it Balbec? It was like being wrung out.

I had *silent* screaming horrors when I landed myself in Clonskeagh Fever Hospital with a temperature over 100 brought on by malnutrition and scarlet fever that caused black spots to dance before my eyes when I was removed in a stretcher from a friend's flat in Northbrooke Road and read off a stone inscription on a gable-end: ASYLUM.

The screaming horrors of Palmerston Park came and went silently too. I lifted my glass of Paddy. The dark wings had flown away. I saw the shapes of bushes in the light that spilled out into the garden and the architectural plans laid out under the Anglepoise and I was calm again. I knew where I was; I had come back to myself; I was among friends.

The Spanish screaming horrors are more sensational and more terrifying, and control is totally lost. I had had a heavy intake of Fundador cognac over an extended period in the great heat of summer in Andalusia, up in the hills in Competa and was sitting on the roof watching the sunset when the attack arrived. It came with the strike of the bell from the church in the square below. I felt it winging through the warm air, aimed at me. Each stroke of the iron clapper was the blow of a bull-whip on my bare back and each stroke laid on with a will by an invisible tormentor. I screamed with pain; each time it struck I howled like a dog.

Could this be Wilde's 'sudden shock' in Reading Gaol, as set out in that long poem of his with its insistent umpah-umpah metrical beat? Kin to the short sharp shock recommended by penal reformers, thundering Tories and heated Whigs all the way back to the shameful stocks, the bawling of perspiring OTC drill-sergeants, cold baths, Queensberry rules and all that bluff camaraderie of sodomy and sadism. Wilde, a 'varsity man himself, would soon have got the hang of it: certainly Lady Wilde, decking out her pet in frocks and frills, had shown little interest in making a man of her little darling. And now came Conal Cullinane, scion of an illustrious line of patriots, bearing tumblers of Paddy on a tray. He was of the pure stock of the most Irish of the Irish, set as a bolt into its socket or a crossbar on two upright goal-posts, rigid as a fundamentalist in his lifelong beliefs (prejudices and bigotries); prey to the heartfelt conviction that of all the countries in the world Ireland was the best and the Irish race uniquely fitted to occupy it.

His father before him had also been a patriot, took up arms to free old Ireland, went on his keeping, conducted his courtship of wife-to-be in ditches and barns, a true patriot and an Irishman through and through, down to his very combinations.

The Bruiser himself had been a fearsome breakaway forward in his Bective Ranger days. He still retained the yachtsman's rolling gait but now in retirement took restricted exercise, knocking buckets of golf balls on the nearby driving-range. Intakes of Paddy gave him a paunch and a jowly look; he liked to have his meals on the table at set times, could be testy if crossed. Formerly he had resembled Ernie O'Mally, hero of the Easter Rising; but now he more resembled Sir Isaac Butt. Conal's face was potato shaped, jowly with a burly burgherish fullness (could it be the fierce intake of Paddy?). There was a hint of brusqueness behind the regular affability, a hint of anger in the *suffused* look. The committed gaping at the TV screen was part of an indulged life; it had made its mark. The Bruiser was a big-beamed, well-set-up, barrel-chested manly type who claimed kinship with Cuchulain, and spoke of bygone times and friends – the Baa Keegan, the Yak and Eskimo Nell, a big American blonde who had caused a stir among the UCD hearties of rugger field and rowing club. The Bruiser's jaw jutted like Dan Dare's.

He watched the RTE news with rapt attention as though World War III were imminent. He liked regular meals in a well-run house where he was boss; was still an active member of the Bective RFU board. Dr Tony O'Reilly, the Heinz bean King and newspaper tycoon, he revered this side idolatry; that an Irishman could perform so brilliantly in an international market appealed to his sense of values, his moral sense of what was what, Irish of the Irish.

Beaming fit to burst he approached bearing two stiff Paddys on a tray with a jug of water for form's sake.

'Get inside this, Rory bach.'

Palmerston Park with its secluded walks, mature pollarded pines with chattering magpies and its flowering magnolia was a popular cruising ground for Dublin gays dropped by the No 12 under the great spread of horse chestnuts at the terminus. The CIE conductors refused to take their fares, fearing herpes contamination: the gays had free rides into the city centre designated *An Lár*.

I was carried in a stretcher into Clonskeagh Fever Hospital and put to bed.

A beady eye had regarded me from the little judas-window set into the door behind which a red night light glowed. Who was that sick bearded person in the bed with just the head showing? If I was anybody, I was a middle-aged woman afflicted with some troublesome female problem.

Assume nothing.

58

Titanic

Two months of relentless pelting rain preceded this Indian summer in September and the patio walls show a greenish tinge where the floodwaters receded. Almost three months have passed since Dervorgilla's departure into Bavaria, but she is expected home from Zug tomorrow. The house is spotless. Giving a last wipe to the mantelpiece Biddy heaves a sigh. 'The first ting Dervorgilla will do is stand at the winda and say "Lord save us!"'

Clinton Binnions, a shadowy form aloft in the cabin of his fast-driven agricultural machine, thunders by a few times, spurning the slopes, fumigating the land, and keeping a close eye on any movements in or around Ballymona Lodge. The word had spread: Mistress Dervorgilla is returning.

Mist obscures the valley below, drifting over the Japanese fence that defines our lot. Lowering itself in the middle as if 'making a leg' or genuflecting, the fence follows the contours of the land, reaching now into the spotlessly cleaned modern bungalow with all its mod cons. The hunt once came this way, a riderless horse galloped by, farting and foaming at the mouth. Sliding doors and both windows are thrown open to the *tic-toc* of little wrens. Summer came in September.

In August five hundred miles south of Newfoundland, at more than 13,000 feet deep, nearly upright on the frigid

Atlantic floor, the *Titanic* was found with all its Edwardian
bric-à-brac intact. The pianos had broken loose, eight cases of
orchids were still there; no sunlight had rotted anything, no
heat had formed algae or parasites to disturb its long rest. The
passengers had in the course of time been devoured by the
denizens of the deep, all 1,513 of them, a banquet in Davy
Jones's locker.

On 14–15 April 1912 it had gone down fatally gashed on its
side, red and green running lights still aglow. It was estimated
that to sink two and a half miles to the ocean bed would have
taken two hours. And what if some sleeping passengers sur-
vived in the dark cabins, awoke to total silence, no human
voices; or perhaps only the deep gurgling of its slow passage
down? What a terrifying end: to be entombed in the fastness
of the ocean deeps, alone, a fate worse than suffocation in the
submarine *Thetis* that sank into the mud of Liverpool Bay with
a whole ship's company that couldn't be raised, to the great
horror of my mother, who was claustrophobic.

On Monday, 1 September Blackie chose a bad day to go
roaming and was run over near Blainroe garage. Cash
Murphy called in person to convey the bad tidings that 'poor
Blackie was kilt'. He had thrown the body into a gripe.

'When Dervorgilla hears this she will do her nut,' Biddy
said. The smell of damp Labrador haunted the porch until
long after Christmas.

Cycled into Wicklow one Wednesday morning to find a drab
line of townspeople with their backs to the wall by Delahunt's
and two gardai on duty directing traffic through.

'What's going on?' I asked a beaky-faced father holding the
hand of his roundy-faced son.

'A funeral.'

This melancholy news was imparted in appropriately
sepulchral tones. They speak of bad weather here as if it were
unusual and not the norm. And here comes the slow black
hearse and the mourners with hands clasped.

To Grand Hotel for lunch of turkey and ham, a glass of Bordeaux. Home the back road, passing surly gum-chewing youth who did not return my salute. Connemara motorists salute pedestrians and passing cyclists by elevating one finger from the steering wheel and tilting the head fractionally to one side.

Dervorgilla gave a weak gasp when told the sad news of Blackie's demise, conveyed with relish by Biddy on the phone. The claw-marks remained on the half-door where he had vaulted out, the sack of Spratts lay in the shed until sold to the Dutchman by penny-pinching Dervorgilla.

We had seen the last of poor Blackie whose remains would begin to decompose in the gripe and be ingested by rats and carrion crows. His powerful pong lingered long in the porch.

Henry Valentine Miller aged eighty interviewed on Radio 4. American intonation of a committed Gauloise smoker, married five times, arrived in Paris aged forty, played ping-pong all his life; plummy actorly voice.

Hushed voice of vain twittery old aunty turns out to be Lawrence (Larry) Durrell, longtime former admirer, the Brit who went to Greece. Effusive praise for *Tropics*, likened to *Lady Chatterley's Lover*, that deeply absurd novel.

Alexandria Quartet sags on the page in a redolent prose limp and pregnant as over-ripe plums. *Balthazar* in paperback among Dervorgilla's few fictions.

Henry Moore passed away last week, aged eighty-eight. As a lad was much affected by Michelangelo's unfinished statue of slaves; praise for M's *monumentality* of vision. Only Blake can speak of vision without causing us embarrassment. The two vain Henrys took their status as Artists very seriously indeed; but only bad ones harp on the fact of being Artists. What is one to make of those big holes cut in monumental blocks of stone? A quite unnecessary complication of the ordinary. Time will do it, an Ice Age; prehistoric standing-stones in a field become scratching posts for cattle, for dogs to piss against.

Teeth paining, gums inflamed, tongue seeks source of pain, capped teeth loose as before treatment, all seething, on fire. Up at 2 a.m. for Anadin. Combine harvesters working in the dark with powerful headlights. Glow of stubble burning in the fields, smoke swirling up; a nocturnal Turner.

7 September

Morning nausea, unable to focus eyesight. Found that left lens has dropped out, resultant head-staggers most unpleasant, Bay of Biscay turmoil; difficulty of finding lens with only one eye. Teeth begin to pain again, joining in worse than before. Very dark stilly night.

8 September

After post set out walking to dental surgeon in Church Road. Empty waiting room. Matthews drained front upper incisor of its poison, extracted pus and blood with powerful finger pressure, a golfer's grip. He is off this weekend for a golfing break near Liverpool. His English friend down with food poisoning. I came at the right time, it could only have got worse, and he would have been away. Prescription for penicillin.

To Old Court Inn for double gin that does not taste of gin. Dowdy bar-girl transformed by new hair-do, and bursting out of her jeans; the sordid old Periwinkle Bar a thing of the past. Renovated premises attract a new type of clientele; gone the boozers of the dark corners, now clean pine surfaces, a reader over from the lending library perusing Rushdie's *Shame* through a monocle, ordering up coffee.

Looked into Taw Shay, thought to be a Provo bar, found an *Independent* reader but no sign of service. The Bridge Tavern gutted by fire. Arson?

Walked home on back road, all uphill. Outline of dead dog on tarmac. Six miles there and back.

My description of my condition had omitted the pain. Matthews drilled a hole into a dead nerve. The pressure building up, he said, penicillin alone would not have cured.

Poor night's rest, no appetite, bottle of white wine. Stillness and darkness of these dry nights.

22 September
Fifteen-mile hike to Greystones by Kilcoole sands, the ghost of Philippa. Took train back, observed by hairy O'Hills the switch-thrower high in his signal-box. Cycled to Barndarrig for gin and tonic with chicken sandwiches at Lil Doyle's. Return mostly on foot, pushing bike, dehydrated, so home more dead than alive, sixteen miles there and back.

At dark the glow of fires in the barley stubble announces the end of summer.

23 September 1986
Guttural foreign (German?) voice on phone this morning announcing that Metz will be in Palma on 27 September, which signals Dervorgilla's imminent return and the end of peace.

Who is this Metz? Mistah Kurtz – he a dead.

59

October Footing

I in a dead man's clothing should be the last person in the world to criticise Colum O'Hills's sartorial get-up. We may speak in the singular, for his clothes never vary, summer or winter, constant as a crow's feathers. My earliest memories are of him dressing. It's a style that came in when clothes rationing went out, in the days of duffel coats.

The Dote that was a worried child has grown into a worried man. Every Sunday he motors down to Mass; no longer a Latin Mass, alas.

The trusty old hacking jacket with single or double vents, pens and pencils protruding from breast pocket, Neolithic trews affording sorry glimpses of blue-white skin like plucked fowl ready for the pot. Down-at-heel brown brogues that have been through miry places, plashy ground. He who detests waste in any form speaks again of his inability to make a garden. The weeds come up again every spring, the *same* weeds that he had uprooted in the previous winter, the *same* stones removed last year are back again this year, apparently burrowing upwards. Gardening books offer 'hundreds of suggestions that are impossible to follow'.

Similarly with the unfinished house which he has been working at sporadically for ten years; it will never be finished; never will he rid himself of all the incompetents; a month's work produces 'an infinitesimal effect'.

My brother's gardening trousers with their layers of scales
and perforations call to mind something very old and loved,
of imperishable lineage: the old bridge at Mostar.

All the fish introduced into the waters of the West are
infected with disease, and sugar beet and wheat with a virus.

Offaly defeated their arch-rivals Galway at Croke Park in
the All-Ireland hurling final. Both counties on either side of
the Shannon had been under six inches of water all summer.
The excitement was so intense that under one Galway stand
(full of priests) a rude toilet collapsed into itself; the Offaly
supporters were in stitches.

The Shannon basin is flooded; root vegetables get scarcer
and dearer as the fields become wetter and wetter; frogs sleep
under every leaf. Fat rats cavort in Dervorgilla's vegetable
patch, nearer home; Biddy lays out poison in the outhouse, in
a saucer.

60

Dusky

Blackie had a younger brother Dusky who had been given by the Dutchman Verveen to the Dorans who rent out Herbsts' gate-lodge to act as guard-dog and pet for Biddy's children. His tenure here on this earth was to be even briefer than his brother's. Dusky made the mistake of *barking too much*. He barked at all who passed on the road, barked at cattle, dogs, passing cars; at the beach he barked at seagulls and at the surf. He barked day and night; chained up in his kennel he continued to bark. He was boisterous in play, barking with excitement, Lara the sly minx setting him on.

One morning Biddy was hanging out the clothes and was sent flying by Dusky; after that his days were numbered. The Quiet Man was told to get rid of him and this he did unobtrusively. One day the kennel was empty. No doubt Dusky had ended his days in a gripe, as his brother before him, both subsumed back into their original elements, bone and gristle become $H_2PO_4 = (OH)$ 20, phosphoric acid and trihydrogen phosphate, hide and teeth become roots and grass, potassium and potash, coal-black Labrador of two years (Blackie) become Anubis, one of the tutelary guardian spirits of the Underworld, become one with Nature.

Had Blackie lived . . . ah. No more would he vault the half-door in the back porch, snore in his dreams, go for the nervous postman who had to make a rapid delivery with

Blackie snarling and snapping at his heels; whimper in Sadie's taxi, scorch after me when I cycled to Brittas or Wicklow, upset all the butchers, challenge a fierce billy-goat tethered on a long chain near the Black Castle during an egg-throwing contest, dribble on the leatherette seat in the Ancient Mariner.

Two wild-looking mountainy men in dungy wellington had appeared at the back door one morning. One looked at Blackie with a twisty eye and pointed a dirty finger. *Datsa de dogge! Datsa de black lad!* He had followed the killer all the way from the dewy killing-field to the kennel at six in the morning, and was accusing Blackie of running lambs and killing a ewe. The bloated farmer stood foursquare on the gravel and looked sideways at Dervorgilla and stated flatly that the dog would have to be put down. Nonsense, Dervorgilla said, Blackie would never kill, and sent them packing, with a flea in their ear.

Enclosed in the back porch and more persistent when the door was closed, the all-pervasive hum of excited wet Labrador persisted long after the demise of Blackie; that strong heartbeat was stilled and his parts decomposing in a gripe near Blainroe garage, by now well digested by rats and carrion crows. That's how matters are settled in the country.

61

Grey Days

O ctober the 7th was a grey day.
I awoke as if drugged from deep sleep. Ned Ward came early to collect Dervorgilla's backbrace and wooden horse from Turkey, her exercise horse.

A classic grey October morning you could say: sky and land as one, Friesians strolling on to the field, clean as if hosed down after the mechanical milking, clean as Peugeots in a Cork car-wash, presently conveying the impression of being airborne, afloat on the milky transparency of an early mist.

On such a morning in Dublin how many years ago had my eldest son (begotten and born in Johannesburg under the fire sign of Cancer) run home, terrified by rough-spoken labourers up to their necks in the drain, laying sewage pipes outside our garden flat in Ranelagh. He had been waiting at the gate for a No. 12 to take him to Miss Kerr's kindergarten in Rathgar when they arrived with their shovels and picks.

He was saved by a sweet girl on the way to her office who took pity on him and brought him in by the gate. Seeing me watching at the narrow window she made a moue to convey, 'I bring him safely back', closing the heavy gate and off with her on her high heels. It was most prettily done and I have never forgotten it; she was so alluring and so kind. Wet grass from overnight rain was trembling in the front garden of 47 Charleston Road; the same blades of grass all atremble in the

morning dew, keen as whetted knives when my middle son
James was born on Shakespeare's Day.

It was on the same sort of grey overcast October days, if
you go back thirty-three years, that I walked a mile to the
Mercy convent in Celbridge, with satchel and school books
and sandwiches, tuppence in my trouser pocket for a Granny
Smith, my mother patting the pocket to make sure the coin
was there. So down the avenue and past the front lodge,
Colum and I, getting our education from the none-too-
tender mercies of the nuns with their straps and rulers and ear-
pulling.

Why does the Bishop give those he confirms a stroke upon
the cheek?

On such a grey morning we sailed from Galway on the
St Edna for Inishere before the three boys were born. Such
overcast days come to remind us of life's brevity and imper-
manence, how our time here on Earth slips away. The cold
Atlantic heaving and gulping with its immense tides, the
clouds passing in the sky, all imply it: this endures, wayfarer,
but you pass.

One such morning a shabby off-white Mini that had never
been through a car-wash came crunching over the gravel, no
longer to set Blackie baying. Colum, come to enquire
whether I would care to accompany him on a business trip to
Laragh to look into a case of suspected arson in the Vale of
Caragh. A Cork publican's summer house had burned down
or been burned deliberately by the owner on the banks of the
Dodder, a little fast-flowing brown stream.

The blackened beams of the two-storey house gutted by
fire were open to the elements; planning permission was
sought to build a new house. But had the rich publican
burned down the old one, the sod?

'Is the water moving?' Colum asked.

'We could have a look.'

I dropped in a twig and it was carried away.

'It's the kind of river that fish like, running over pebbles,'
my brother said, standing on a tussock and staring down.

There were no fish in the shallow fast-flowing brown stream.
On an ash tree by the overgrown driveway a sign said
FERRETS SOLD.

Driving back at breakneck speed as always Colum remarked upon the strange yet typical greyness of those autumn
days. Days that seem to turn one inside out. 'Typical' was a
strong word in his vocabulary and could work both ways,
conveying either mild approbation or severe censure. For
such a patient man, he drove like a maniac, impatient to get
from one point to another with the minimum of time wasted,
for he hated wasting time, of which he seemed to have so
little not occupied by working, generally overtime.

So we went hurtling along the narrow lanes. Were he to
hit anything, going at this speed, we were goners, pulverised.

'And herself, how is she?'

'Stella doesn't believe in breathing.'

Stella was way out. One of her speculations was: Do we
breathe the same air as the air in Julius Caesar's time?

'That's bad. We have to breathe.'

'I know.'

'I saw a nun walking backwards up a hill the other day,' I
said. 'Walking very slowly backwards up the hill. What does
it signify?'

'I don't know. Indigestion?'

'Is Stella still reading Eudora Welty in the clothes cupboard
with the cat?'

'Oh yes.'

'And the jackdaws – how are they making out?'

'They all died.'

Stella doesn't believe in breathing. Can you beat it? Time
arrested is the stillness of nature. Stillness helps thought but
thought itself is helpless. Arthur Miller, uniquely self-
pervaded, is having *Death of a Salesman* done into Chinese. 'I
won't take the rap' will be rendered into Chinese as 'I will not
carry the charred cooking-pot on my back.'

Turkeys are fed and thrive on dandelions on the Beltons'

farm. Chickens absolutely love dandelions. You can tell the eggs laid by hens fed on dandelions. Wednesday is killing day.

The bullfinch has become a protected species under Section 19 of the Wild Life Act of 1976.

62

Verveen

One day I was in O'Connor's buying slices of turkey and stepping out who did I see but Franz Verveen the Dutchman standing under the Mona Lisa's smirk and invited him to step into Healy's pub that was conveniently adjacent with its door hospitably thrown open. So in with us for a few jars.

In the dim convivial atmosphere Verveen lost some of his ceremonial Dutch reserve. He was not a man you would care to be overly familiar with, nor could I ever imagine myself addressing him as Franz. He borrowed some of the sheets I had just run off at the copying machine. He bred Labradors; Blackie and Dusky had come from the Verveen kennels. I questioned him about Jan Cramer. I told him I had worked with the puppets in Amsterdam and indeed had met the famous Harry Tussenbruck, the doll-maker. Imagine that, now. I knew the famous old repertory cinema with the impossible Dutch name there by the canal and had drunk Bols gin. As a Piscean I could not but love a small city with so many canals running through it. We got along fine, Franz Verveen and I. Later that night I phoned his number and the wife answered.

'You don't know me from Adam,' I began diplomatically.

'Oh but I *do* know you from Adam, Mr Rory of the Hills. And what I want to know is, what have you done with my poor Frow? He has retired to bed with a most thick head on him. He wishes to convey a message. He liked the pages you showed him and suggests you offer it to the *Wicklow People*.'

Time does not exactly fly in Ballymona Lodge. Two months of driving rain gave way to an Indian summer in September and not a dry day since St Swithin's prior to that. A great Soviet-style grass-cutting machine with shadowy driver aloft in his high cabin spewed out silage in the Carmelite Missionary grounds in an August infested with flies. Time passes as it must have passed for the Good Fairy in the Pooka's pocket.

Many old walled gardens have snails. For this you need a pair of hedgehogs to sort out the snails; the patient crunching of snail shells hour after hour on a soft summer's day has been going on for fifteen billion years. Think on that, browsers.

63

The Mangle

I was a skinny child, a faddy eater, timid, afraid of my shadow. Notoriously faddy at home in my own habitat and in familiar surroundings; away from home I was impossible, the despair of my parents, and had to be coaxed to eat anything, could hardly be induced to swallow a mouthful.

'Now we'll have no more of this nonsense!' would give way to 'Leave the child alone, don't *nag* at him'; but neither threats nor cajoleries worked. I was a neurotic wreck, fearing bouncing girls as I would soldiers in uniform; Dr O'Connor prescribed a tonic, iron. I would not eat butter.

Luncheon with my parents and the Dote in the Royal Hibernian Hotel was an ordeal of the first magnitude that began at the revolving door with uniformed flunkey in white gloves saluting us as we walked in. I felt completely at a loss; the aromas of the Grade A hotel ambience were as unsettling as incense at Benediction and a bishop chanting in Latin; it turned my stomach. I wanted to go home and get behind the mangle where I felt safe.

Stiff and awkward in my best suit and new shoes and hair stiffened with conditioner at Maison Prost in Stephen's Green I felt ashamed to speak, too timid to eat or even attempt this display of unfamiliar dishes. Secretly I said to myself: What are we doing here?

'Ma,' I whispered. 'I don't like it here. I want to go home.'

'Nonsense, dotey. This is a lovely place,' my mother replied in her richest, plummiest voice, smelling of cognac and tobacco.

When we were all seated, after the Removal of the Overcoats, and my mother's fur all drenched in perfume, her hat and demi-veil removed, we were faced with a huge menu in French and the *maître d'hôtel* to explain the mysteries, familiarly addressed as Charlie by my parents. The waists of the young waitresses were cinched in by shiny black leather belts which made their bottoms stick out and they wore maids' white caps with ruffed black bands like garters inverted coquettishly on their nodding heads. They swayed on their feet as they approached, bending over the table to spoon soup into our plates from a great tureen, their made-up faces set stiff in artificial smiles from lips that seemed to bleed.

I scarcely recognised my parents in their posh city clothes, my mother's voice up a pitch, my father's down, when they spoke to Charlie or 'our' waitress, but between themselves they murmured in soft asides, commenting on the diners around them. I picked at what was put before me while the Dote ploughed through his meal.

'I want to go home, Ma.'

'We'll be out of here soon, pet. Your father has to settle the bill. We'll go to Combridge's. You'd like that.'

'I want to get in behind the mangle, Ma.'

John Sibley, a benevolent portly man, owned Combridge's in Grafton Street and sold books there; he played left-handed off a handicap of eight in Greystones and was known to my parents, who seemed to know everybody in Ireland living and dead. His hands were strong and stubby and fragrant with Cologne, the nails clipped short. He set the book in the centre of the wrapping paper, shot his cuffs, squared it off neatly, smiling a tight smile, a magician about to perform a conjuring trick, then he brought the overlap down in two v's, tucked them in at either end, Sellotaped the parcel, tied it up with string which he broke with a quick jerk and handed the package to me with a wink.

'Don't we say "Thank you"?' my mother asked.

'Thank you,' I whispered, mesmerised by this jugglery.

In the art shop at the corner of Molesworth Street and Kildare Street I chose some Winsor & Newton brushes and watercolours in tubes (Hookers Green No. 2, Burnt Sienna, Cobalt Blue) which my mother again paid for. I was much too timid to ask prices or pay for anything I bought.

The heavy mangle stood in the kitchen between the tall cupboard and the window under the clothes line. Blocky as a medieval torture instrument oozing black grease it stood foursquare in wrought iron on its castors; the space between it and the wall was used regularly by the cats as their lavatory, the old messes growing fuzzy hair. When the stink became unendurable old Mrs Henry, our cook, cleaned it out with buckets of water and Jeyes Fluid.

When I hung on to the mangle for dear life I felt safe. Nothing could get at me in there, skinny as a skeleton.

64

A Hanging

Aged about ten I dug a hole six feet deep in the soft soil of the cleared potato patch in the garden and then spread and raked the earth tidily about the hole, opened out the *Evening Mail* and held it tight as a drum with bricks at four corners. Then I bet my younger brother sixpence that he couldn't jump on it without tearing it.

'You're on! It's a cinch.'

Brother Colum, the Dote, two years my junior and already a very serious person, removed his boots, peeled off jacket and pullover to make for the lightest of landings, light as a feather, even executed a couple of 'soft' trial jumps on the raked part as rehearsals for the unimaginably soft landing that would earn him the tanner.

I threw the silver coin down by the hidden pit and stood back with folded arms.

'Go ahead, chump. Let's see you then.'

With a look of intense concentration my brother jumped on to the centre of the innocently spread paper. The winner's smirk was wiped from his face as he landed and descended and descended; his feet told him there was nothing there and down he went, accelerating horribly, as the felon swinging on a rope, a plumbline dropping vertical into unheard-of depths, down into the very bowels of the earth itself.

The fixed expression of pure shock was indeed striking.

And a muffled cry came up from below where I had packed straw.

'Not fair!'

65

On Cuesta del Cielo

Some years before and Rory of the Hills was living at Nerja, first on Calleo Carabeo and then on Calle de las Angustias, at forty-eight the father of three bouncing boys; and had taken to tramping the grand asphodel-clad valleys between there and Frigiliana with Augpick and Kit Horner with his Jew's harp and bush boots and wine *bota*, three fellows hairy as Mormons, bearded to the very eyes.

And later again with Augpick when we moved to Competa up in the foothills of the Sierra Almijara and together walked the logging trails that led back into the hills, never finding the legendary fish-trail to Granada. These I declare among the pleasantest times I spent anywhere at any time with anybody ever.

Augpick has broken his under-jaw, the inferior maxilla, when being driven, a 'trusted mechanic' at the wheel, to a fancy-dress party in Halifax. The car overturned on a tight corner. Augpick was encased in a suit of armour like a small sardine in a tin; when the helmet snapped shut away went poor Cyril's lower jaw.

Thereafter the jaw gave him a permanently pike-like undershot truculent look, which he played up to with snooty Danish door-keepers, Spanish major-domos and *maîtres d'hotel* whom he treated in the most high-handed manner imaginable.

Augpick would call at seven in the morning and we had coffee and *anis seco* at the bar at the end of Calle Carabeo and then down with us on to the dried-up Rio Chilar for the walk to the electrical power station and from there on to the lower aqueduct for easy walking on aqueduct walls a foot and a half wide; an hour's walk took us to the upper Morisco viaduct that meandered back off into the hills. Booster *Bustaid* was sold at the *farmacia*, and two of these would set us off, inhaling joints or taking hash on bread to send us merrily on our way. By midday we would be back in the high hills, taking tuna and tomato lunch on a high corner of the viaduct in the breeze among pines, the *bota* chilling in the water, the breeze blowing up from below.

We went as far as we could on a day's march, turning for home in the cool of the evening to the sigh of the breeze in the pines and the tinkle of the goat-bells below, the unseen goat herd clacking his tongue at them; to reach Frigiliana as the light faded in the sky, to sup in the plaza near the church. And then the last leg by road by La Molinetta to reach Nerja at nightfall.

Often we walked to the deserted village of the copper miners, just the walls standing, in the shade of a great palm tree. Kit took a 'short-cut' and Augpick and I lost him down in a valley of young pines, then in the remote distance we saw a tiny figure on the skyline and heard the distant Jew's harp; Kit twanged it and crossed over into another valley, coming off the higher aqueduct.

Often, drinking on the Nerja *paseo* at the Alhambra or Marissal, we spoke of climbing Cuesta del Cielo. It was no more a climb than ascending the Big Sugarloaf in Co. Wicklow; but a long hike upwards to the summit over 2,000 feet high. So one day in winter we did it.

Kit Horner, Cyril Augpick of Halifax, Nova Scotia, Old Parr and Rory of the Hills set off early on foot past La Luna shrouded in early morning mist. Some hours later we approached the summit. The ground cover of rosemary and thyme and tussocky scutch grass that scented the air gave way to scree and bare sandstone outcrop that stank of sulphuric acid when broken off. When I stepped across one such tussock something halted me. I knelt, parted the grass, looked down into a hole dark and evidently bottomless. A stale, spent muggy air blew up from the innards of the mountain.

'Hear me! You hear me down there?' I called down into the great dank silence and darkness below.

I felt the cool breeze blowing off the summit and my sweat turned cold and I held up my right hand like a traffic cop and said 'Stop where you are!' to Old Parr who was labouring up the mountainside with the sweat fairly pouring off him, Moses toting those heavy Tablets of the Law, my call halting him in his tracks.

'What is it? A snake? a fairy rath? an apparition?'

'A turd?' suggested Kit Horner.

'A hole,' I said.

'A *hole*?'

'A hole 2,000 feet deep,' I said.

'Ah-hah.'

I must have stepped over the ventilation exit of the long-abandoned copper mine; the miners had not thought fit to seal it up, an air vent so small and so high up on the side of the mountain where no one walked. I found a round rock the size of a cannonball and dropped it into the dark maw open wide as a man's shoulders; it fell away as if suddenly sucked down into the blackness below that seemed to breathe or to hold its breath, waiting.

After an interminably protracted silence − for it was still falling − we heard the reverberations 2,000 feet below as the projectile struck the floor of the mine, echoing up from a great dank deserted chamber long abandoned by the copper miners.

'Ehhue,' snickered Augpick who was kneeling beside me. 'That's fukken deep, man.'

We moved on up to the summit, the sweat drying on us. If one, not looking too carefully, had stepped into it, the fall would have been ghastly as a hanging; that eternity between the hangman's grunt announcing the springing of the trap, when the poor hanged bugger's weight carried him abruptly downwards with a remorseless gravitational pull that severed his spinal column. This ghastly fall would have taken longer. The luckless rambler howling as he descended would be scratching and tearing at the sides as he was sucked downwards.

We sat about a cairn of cut rocks on the summit and rolled joints and brought out the tuna, tomatoes and bread, and the chilled vodka and orange juice from the *bota*, and we disposed ourselves there at our ease.

'*Mejor no hay,*' declared Kit Horner, inhaling deeply until he was cross-eyed. '*Hay no haya novedad.*'

He stared wildly about him with that manic look of his, the trapped animal look you encounter behind bars in a zoo.

'On a clear day I dare say you can see Africa,' said Old Parr, the Grim Old Grouser. 'The tops of the Atlas.'

It's difficult to embarrass a Spaniard but it can be done, Jim Parry told me once. I had embarrassed Placido Espejo by attempting to speak of abstract matters when in my cups; but for an Andalusian the abstract does not exist; only the concrete is real. *Realidad* is a rock, all else presumption.

It is clearly impossible for my brother to suffer humiliation; for his Taoist patience and reserve puts him beyond that. Once in Kensington Gardens near the monument he had his hand on the door of an unoccupied phone-booth when an angry drunk tore it from his grasp and shouldered him aside, and my brother with a weak smile gave him best. It was the same sheepish, deferential smile he had given the haughty horsewoman, asking was her mount nervous. 'No, but it's a spooky kind of day,' the lady said.

We are what we seem to be. The man from Halifax, Nova Scotia; the man from Hounslow West, home of howling dogs; the man from Murri in India; the man from Michigan, USA, making church pews from pitch pine in a garage near Crystal Palace, with power-line plugged into the mains. And Rory of the Hills.

66

The Road to Aranjuez

The distance from Cape Cod to Jaffa is
terrible – and yet not so great.

Jeremiah Stone

The car was a grey-blue BMW about 1970 vintage, an
intermittently sound two-litre model with 100,000
miles on the clock (another 2,000 would be added
after the journey from Garratt Lane to Competa and back,
or near the distance from London to Moscow) which Parry
had procured for a modest price, deviously arrived at, from
Pablo the Asturian, an economist from Barcelona now
working for Lloyds Bank International and living in Saffron
Walden.

The trip began at the Jolly Gardener in Garratt Lane near
the Crystal Palace with the BMW parked outside, ice melting
in the gin and tonic balanced on the bonnet, and Parry's
soiled plimsolls sticking out under the chassis as he patiently
tinkered with a faulty king-pin on the sunny morning we set
off for Spain where the consummate auto engineer would
spend much time on the flat of his back under the engine with
never a word of complaint from him.

We just made it to the Dover ferry.

Then the great engines were churning up mud and seaweed from the harbour and the clumsy vessel nudged away by
tugs was reversing out of Dover harbour, when a wit remarked 'They're trying to raise Lord Lucan.'

We fasted across the Channel and down through the
cheesy centre of France and all the way to Hendaye with our

useless pesetas, except for three Mars bars on credit in a garage somewhere near Parthenay.

The BMW kept breaking down and Parry was on the flat of his back again. As a non-driver I took the passenger seat and stayed awake, attempting to keep the driver alert and diverted. Old Parr, foodless for two days, was grumpy as a sealion; Parry fast asleep on the back seat, worn out by hunger, long stints at the wheel and more and more spells on the flat of his back, tinkering with the engine. Somewhere on the long straight *carretera* south of Madrid the engine mounting broke when we drove off the road.

Both of them were reliable drivers, and now it was Old Parr's stint at the wheel, while Parry slept in the back seat. Getting no response from some witticism, I glanced at the driver: both hands lightly touched the steering wheel, the BMW was going at a fair lick down the motorway, the driver's chin on his chest and his eyes closed, fast asleep.

'*¡Cuidado!*' I whispered.

But now he was elsewhere, sound asleep; the BMW holding its level course. If my blood had run cold before, it froze now, for approaching us at high speed was a mighty pantechnicon coming on heavy and dangerous as a battle-tank going into action, the driver's face just a blur aloft in his cabin behind the bug-smeared windscreen, staring down aghast as the BMW left the road and Old Parr was instantly wide awake. The BMW plunged into a boulder-strewn gully fortunately clear of boulders for some way, with the huge pantechnicon – I saw a blurred *Huesca* – roaring alongside, releasing mighty air-brakes; we rode up the gully for a moment of pure terror and then Old Parr regained the *carretera* and presently brought the car to a trembling halt and Parry wide awake now was asking what the hell was going on.

It was not the first or last time that death had stared me in the face in the company of Old Parr, who was becoming more and more irascible as the years rolled on, the old fart.

That was the night when he went sleepwalking and spoke in tongues – Urdu or Punjabi. The Grim Reaper who had touched him lightly on the shoulder somewhere south of Madrid now bore him backwards into the first language of his childhood in India before the Parrs sailed for England, carried him back to a time when as a toddler he had prattled in Urdu.

He spoke to me in that tongue, handing me a heavy key, laughed a light skittering laugh fit for another language, a strange tongue, and I seemed to hear bare feet pattering across a hot courtyard, the monsoon blowing in the tamarinds and a dark servant bowing obsequiously to the Sahib.

I put him to bed, still tittering and muttering to himself, safely tucked up on his foam mattress bed in Calle Rueda above the hill-village overlooking the cemetery whose columbariums gleamed white as bones in the moonlight under the scudding clouds.

(Later reports of the Missing Lord had it that he was alive and well and now resident in Ontario, Canada, after brief sojourns in Australia and Botswana.)

Some years previous to this I was the passenger in a Seat hired from Pepe Angel with Old Parr again at the wheel and Kit Horner, never the most reliable of drivers, snoring on the back seat. Alert and wide awake our nerves were ajangle, as nerves tend to be after an outing with Kit; for we had been walking around Granada in teeming rain, drinking great quantities of vodka and shooting pool until the early hours of the morning; now we were on our way back to Nerja.

We seemed to be passing through an illusionary landscape on the way to Malaga in pouring rain with earthen embankments collapsing on both sides, little or no traffic passing either way, an unearthly desert like the sequences in negative film stock in *Orphée* where black becomes white and vice versa.

For quite some time I had been seeing white rats flitting across the washed-out road, coming from the earthworks that had been softened up and fallen into the road; they came mostly from my side and disappeared under the wheels. I did not mention these rats to Old Parr, who drove in silence.

It was the silence in *The Turn of the Screw* movie announcing the appearance of the dead Quint on the battlements. All nature had become woozy and shapeless and had fallen silent and into this we glided slow as glue, as ahead of us the white rats flitted, ignored by the driver wrapped in thought.

We rounded a sharp turn and there with Madrid number plates was a long black limousine half off the road, suspended in the void, the front wheels – a daring cinematic touch – still turning, the headlights probing the valley across which heavy rain fell in torrents, bombarding our roof.

Old Parr sucked in his breath and pulled in some way ahead and we walked back without a word to where a shadowy form – male – slumped over the wheel.

Old Parr pulled open the door on the driver's side, no doubt preparing himself for a grisly sight; but the car was empty. The headlights were on and the wheels turning; behind the outline of the shiny black car the murky sky was lit up by the light of the city we had left, backed by the snowcapped Sierra Nevada.

67

Saul Bellow Reading at TCD

12 October

To Dublin by train with Old Parr to hear Saul Bellow reading a paper at the Edmund Burke Hall in Trinity. Bought Penguin *To Jerusalem and Back* – Bellow's only non-fiction – at Hanna's for the author to sign. Hall packed, seating 400. Proceedings start on time for a change. Professor Thomas Kilroy of University College Galway leads the distinguished American guest on to the podium. Bellow dark-visaged, smaller than anticipated, formally dressed in suit, looks younger than his seventy years and cannot decipher some of his own notes dashed off in flight with maybe a stiff drink to hand. 'The Mind of the Reader & the Expectations of the Writer in America', a fine rolling title.

The great minter of punchy phrases is in splendid form. He speaks of words going home – in the sense of hitting the bull's eye – of psychobabble (did he invent this term?), of 'the dark menace of complexity'. He is an expert fielder of awkward questions from the floor; cranes forward to listen carefully with manic half-smile; Saul Bellow does not cosy up.

Applause goes on and on at the end, but Bellow and his minders retire to a back room. Old Parr would not hear of me going there to have my copy signed, and a chance to shake the great man's hand, having read everything that Bellow published since *Dangling Man* of 1944. Penguin New Writing had published an article on young American writers attending some conference where Mailer, Baldwin, Updike, Terry Southern and Styron had pontificated. Bellow – a pale face with pimples, long-suffering Talmudic eyes – had remained with his buddies in a corner, telling dirty stories. I had liked the cut of his jib even then; but I never got to meet him or to shake his honest hand. An abstracted Banville went out with his wife among the press of Bellow's admirers leaving the lecture hall.

I took Old Parr to my father's speakeasy in Lower Georges Street, the Long Hall, to drink some fine old malt, on which subject – fine malts – he was an authority. And so back to Ballymona Lodge with pork chops on the evening train by the tossing sea.

68

An Incident on the
Road to Pontoon

Once in the August twilight near Lake Cong with a corncrake calling in the valley below us Rosita and I filled with Jameson and illegal poteen liberally bestowed by the Roche brothers and it hid in bottles in a hayshed and we were put on the wrong road on hired bicycles by the younger and wilder Roche brother and found ourselves going hell for leather on a switchback Mayo back road white and dusty in the moonlight and becoming trickier and trickier as the swooping descents gave way to steeper and steeper ascents one giving impetus to the other until I applied the brakes and found there were none and then came a steep descent followed by an even steeper one followed by a sharp turn and no longer listening to the corncrake I skidded into a western wall surmounted by rusty barbed wire and almost went through the wall or it through me and had I been less sozzled and incapacitated the wall or the barbed wire together might have done me serious injury but the skid helped to modify some of the impact but fucked me into the barbed wire anyway.

Rosita cycled back to disentangle me from the barbed wire and helped me into the homestead in Pontoon fortunately not far off, I bleeding profusely and put to bed with the fleas that made a night of it, sucking the blood of the wounded cyclist.

Next morning Rosita cycled to the hotel at the head or end

of Lough Cong for a bottle of Jameson and called on Dr O'Leary.

I was sitting up in the flea-ridden bed in extreme discomfort with nose and left kneecap swollen to twice their size when the younger Roche arrived in his green postal van to say he had a telegram for himself, stained like a Redskin with flea bites and camomile lotion and iodine swabs. The telegram from London said: CONGRATULATIONS YOU HAVE WON THE AMERICAN-IRISH FOUNDATION GRANT WORTH $7000.

Old Parr was to join us later in teeming rain, sharing one modernised cottage with thatched roof, later gutted by arson, a grudge against Johnny O'Toole by a local Borstal Boy had it in for him. This would have been in 1977 or thereabouts.

Old Parr was the very man who had unsoberly, following our bout of wine-imbibing with Nagenda, driven his Citroën Diane into a wide deep hole dug by road-menders directly outside the police station at Clapham Junction; I again in the passenger seat, with old Parr's wife's baroque cello (1792) wrapped up like a mummy and propped against the back seat, a shrouded louring presence guarding us.

'Mr Parr, we are not disputing whether or not the hole was lit or signposted; we are considering the fact that you were breathalysed and found to be twice above the normal limit. I am fining you £50 and withdrawing your licence for one calendar year. Case dismissed. Next.' So spoke the Beak.

Old Parr, I may say, ate humble pie. This would have been a couple of years earlier, around '75.

69

A Walk to Greystones

Something is always happening in Binnions's long sloping field; or beyond in the valley, or along the skyline. The living room changes with the seasons, as does the valley outside; freezing produces Japanese snow effects on the glass. Sunlight then gives bathyscope luminosity of summer sunlight refracted on ceiling when filtered through batten curtains and double glazing, shadows of rowan saplings dance on ceiling, producing those seabed effects, spurts of deliquescent transparency. Added to if anything when hungover, seen from sofa, shivering *nell' intracta foresta*.

27 October
To dispel hangover I walked the fifteen miles from the Murrough or plain-by-the-sea along the railway line to Greystones whose cosseted canine population is growing. To Burnaby Hotel for foaming pint. Last swallows of the year flit over Gents' Bathing Place, *sans* diving board. Saw bullfinch in bush. Grim Protestant ladies of advanced years and stern deportment out stalking behind small yapping dogs that befoul promenade. The ex-racing driver (Isle of Man) Manliff Barrington seen darting into newsagent's for his *Irish Times*. A wedding reception in full swing at La Touche Hotel, Eire Nua strongly represented, excited bridesmaids being photographed. Priest displaying social ease with hands in pockets.

Bemused horse standing by a dead horse at Blacklion cross-roads. Full tide in harbour. Fishermen asprawl on boulders.

16 November
Chill clear November day. Sickle moon, lights of Dungans-town west across the valley, Ballinaclash beyond, Rathdrum.
   Knorr vegetable soup with dash of sherry topped with dab of cream. Cheese omelette and Mateus Rosé, Mouton Cadet. We do ourselves proud in Ballymona Lodge.

70

An Official Visit:
Garda Reynolds

22 November

Sweet sounds of early morning in the wood, a pheasant's choked-off cry, a ship's siren out at sea. Postal van at nine, sound of letters arriving, my limited contact with outside world. Slow procession of grey clouds over horizon; Basho image of thoroughly Japanese snow mountain in the far distance serenely bathed in early afternoon light. Preparing supper. Pork fillet tenderised with judicious blows of rolling-pin, bombarded with seasoning, garlicky and ready for fan oven, mashed spuds rigid with garlic, G&T appetiser, claret at the meal. Orson Welles, peerless trencherman, said the way to appreciate food was to eat it alone and think about each mouthful. Pass the salt.

Sky is similar to October Competa sky, mussel-blue shapes clearly defined, reddish distant hills, evening star shining bright in damp clear air. In half an hour all will change.

Friday, 28 November

Biddy in her element this morning bringing authentically tragic news. Had I heard what happened in the night just over the hill? I hadn't? Well, hear this. A mother and daughter were raped and strangled, or vice versa, strangled and then raped the almost naked mother in the living room and the daughter, aged twenty-four, dispatched in the kitchen, the

Nolan family wiped out.

In the shed the rats had taken the poison and were now dying in convulsions in the foundations. The louring afternoon brought a rare visitor in the shape of a well-fed Civic Garda with notebook and pencil and some queries about my movements in the last few days. Garda Reynolds.

I invited him in. He sat on the edge of the sofa alongside his cap, getting me in a good light, refusing Nescafé or tea or a drink, all patent bribes. He hoped I didn't mind him putting some questions, it was only a formality. My movements now (licking the point of his pencil, arranging his great posterior): would I mind telling him what I was doing on Tuesday, on Wednesday at such-and-such an hour, where was I, could I say now?

I cycled to Brittas on Wednesday to Cullen's shop and spoke to Una. And returned when, and who saw me and who talked to me, if anybody? I saw none, none spoke to me, I said.

The large phlegmatic presence fills the room to overflowing. I had a drink at McDaniel's and spoke to John Stamp who served me. Back when? Just at dark. That would be (shooting cuff to check wristwatch) 4.30? Right. And didn't stay long? No (no light on bike). Don't mention rat poison, as I was tempted to do, in the way of tittle-tattle; don't mention bike without light, don't pick up heavy fire-dogs, don't fiddle, sit perfectly still, look innocent, I picked up the heavy fire-iron and laid it down again with a sickly smile. The Garda licked the point of his pencil. Had I seen anyone acting suspicious?

I wrote books bedad, had I by any chance any of them here and could he see one? I had three sons, had I, and a wife in London? Now he is reading the back flap of *Balcony of Europe* listing *Last Exit to Brooklyn*, *Cain's Book*, *Tropic of Cancer*, all dirty books brought out by Calder and all banned in the Republic. Had I written any of these? Now he is dipping into *Balcony* as though sifting incriminating evidence, licking the lead and frowning. It's not looking too good.

He has been stationed here eight years. No, no leads yet. Mrs Nolan was a widow aged sixty years, a widow eight years. After aeons of agonising time, slow time, the Garda put away his notebook, thanked me and took his leave.

The squad car was parked up the road. He had come on foot with his cap on, wearing his stern official face.

On 12 December the *Irish Times Anthology* launch was held at the Castle Inn on Lord Edward Fitzgerald Street above Dublin Castle, attended by all the hoi polloi among whom was Liam Miller of Dolmen Press, Kavanagh's widow seated in a corner, Maeve Binchy smiling amid her crush of admirers; seen prominently too was the undershot pike's jaw of Francis Stuart of *Black List H* fame, instantly recognisable for what Bellow wickedly called 'the cynosure flush', applied to some mobster. Among the contributors was Rory, instantly set upon by a furious woman who lit into him because of some remark let drop some sixteen years before in Berlin. I had no recollection of this furious woman or that indiscreet remark; how tenaciously we Irish hang on to our grudges!

On the following morning I happened to be passing through Chapelizod *en route* to the bar by the bridge and coming out of the newsagent's with a copy of the *Irish Times* found myself in bearded profile on the front page. Rory of the Hills at Castle Inn.

It was the very day on which Fortune, the murderer of the Nolans, was brought to trial. Perpetua in a froth of excitement phoned Dervorgilla, screeching down the line 'He's on the front page of the *Irish Times*!' Was her sister harbouring a double murderer? The report of the brief court hearing was below the picture: bearded pard in foxy profile holding a dirty roll-up in one murderous claw. Dervorgilla had kittens.

The *Wicklow People* was sold out by midday. YOUTH ACCUSED OF MURDERING WOMEN, ran the restrained headline in a news-sheet more accustomed to reporting cow winched to safety, having toppled off a cliff.

Meanwhile Rory was ordering up a half of Guinness and a Jameson chaser.

Barman Stamp very smart in a new red gansey pulled half a pint for me at McDaniel's that same afternoon and said 'Hanging is too good for that fucker.'

'What about half-hanging him?' I suggested. 'You know, *half-hang* him. Then cut him down, bury him, leave him under for a bit, to meditate on his crimes. Then dig him up and re-hang him. Like marinating snipe.'

John Stamp's eyes blazed.

'Now by God you're talking!'

'Or do the job properly. Give him the works. Crucify him. That's a gorgeous gansey you've got on.'

Tommy Cullen, a decent sober man, at age fourteen picked up a detonator at the Arklow mines to have it blow up in his face: he lost the sight of one eye. Years later, now married, a one-eyed father, he was to lose a much-loved son, buried him in the ground.

Storm wind for a few hours, then dying out. Fire in living room dying out, wood and coal mixed. Gunshot at dusk. Two figures hurrying across Binnions' field now empty of Friesians.

All stations jammed, only Spanish clear as a bell, barometer reading 55 degrees, biting wind, crows blown hither and thither, gulls tossed about in clear blue sky before sunset; fire long dead in grate. A rake of drunken tinkers were boozing by the stream that runs past the Forge pub. A drunken male attacking an even drunker slut.

The skin of the murdered daughter was found in Fortune's fingernails, Doran the bus driver informs me; now how does he know that? How the news gets around.

71

Halley's Comet

'Are the Chinese a shy race? What do you suppose?' Stella Veronica speaks in suddenly inspired *non sequiturs*; she exists on a different wavelength to you and I.

'Shynese,' Colum titters.

They had been married thirty-six years. Their nuptials were celebrated in Brompton Oratory in winter; a fellow thirsting for the sacrament tried to shoulder them aside and a moth trapped in a candle flame was immolated on the spot. Her three ravishing sisters were bridesmaids. The newly-weds lived in Ludlow Road out Ealing way, like so many Irish before them.

They were very formal with each other. She was most withdrawn; deeply withdrawn within herself, and a past-mistress of the nubilous aside. As for my brother, you would suppose the next wind would blow him away.

I recall a man with baby-blue eyes in the Prince of Wales in Highgate who introduced himself as the grandson of Douglas Hyde. Just behind us in Pond Street was the summer residence of Oliver Cromwell.

In a snug in Castlebar in Mayo run by two dumpy old women who crouched in the window-ledge like Rhode Island Reds on their perch, observing movements on the road, the cornerboys clustering and cat-calling; the two old ones now and again retreating into a dark recess in the rear. A small fierce old man with crutches by his tall stool sipped Jameson and kept watching me, at last addressed me, asking the one question to which there is no satisfactory answer: 'What do you do?'

'I write books actually.'

'What classa books?'

'Books that don't sell.'

He had driven a cab for years in the Bronx and advised me to go there and study the low life, there was plenty of it in the Bronx. Later, looking for the Gents, I entered a room full of shelves packed with biscuit tins, the man from the Bronx was sitting on the edge of a camp-bed in carpet slippers, preparing to retire.

'We're all in a glasshouse now.'

Where was I?

And where am I now? What do you do when memory begins to go? As soon as I'm fitted with a bridge my potency will begin to go. Seas, rivers, lakes, great bodies of water always in motion will no longer stimulate me. Formerly woken by an erection (the cock that is the herald to the morn) and now thank God hardly a stir down there. The pictures on the wall have taken a slide.

I spend too much time looking back into the past; and the past that I know is no longer there; it has taken a slide, God knows where. I too have taken a slide.

'Time flies when you're enjoying yourself,' Biddy called out the other day, bringing her household chores to a triumphant conclusion. 'Throw on your jacket and I'll give you a lift into town.'

Lara is just like her ma, with the same taste for the melodramatic.

'Herbst's bull broke out!'

'Mammy can't go to Spain!'

'Laurence is lost!'

Halley's comet, now at its closest, is coming around again,

returning in the time-span of one human life, and will be forty million light years away in March when I turn fifty-nine on the 3rd.

As it whips past the sun it discards ice and star dust, dragging a peacock tail seventy million miles long. Its mysterious icy heart is said to hold clues to the origin of our solar system.

It was seen by Julius Caesar, aged seventeen, above Gaul in 87 BC. And the infant Eudora Welty was carried in her sleep to the window of her home in North Congress Street, Jackson, Mississippi, by her father Christian Welty to see it. She was always waked for eclipses and grew up to the striking of clocks. Her mother had been born left-handed and stuttered; in her family were five left-handed brothers, a left-handed mother and a father who could write with both hands at the same time, also backwards and forwards and upside down, different words with each hand. He had a telescope with brass extensions to find the moon and the Big Dipper.

Was Halley the clever savant who pulled or pushed Tsar Nicholas backwards and forwards in a wheelbarrow through a hedge in the garden of some English lord when the Tsar visited England (useful footnotes to history), unless I confuse him with another?

A chilly winter here as in England where the bats have miscarried along the Somerset borders. The Shannon has burst its banks at Athlone.

72

Dervorgilla at Home

No tenemus nada . . . Yo soy nada.
Honduran proverb. (We are nothing; I am nothing.)

In a brown dressing-gown drab as a Benedictine shroud Dervorgilla prepares to retire for the night after a good long souse in the tub, the bathroom being the only room in the home unreachable by phone. She asked to see the story I had just finished, one well calculated to set feminists' teeth on edge. She would take it to bed with her; it might send her to sleep. Next morning I had her comment.

'People sometimes ask me what kind of writing you do. I tell them "Writing without beginning, middle or end." It *still* has no beginning, middle or end.'

'By the first third of the next century, which will be loudly pictorial, writers may become extinct,' I said. 'As the dodo, the corncrake, Steller's sea-cow, bell-ringers and town-criers, our trade will be as extinct as falconry.'

Yeats in his old age wrote: 'I am a crowd, I am a lonely man; I am nothing.' And again: 'In a little time places may begin to seem the only hieroglyphs that cannot be forgotten.' A prehistoric standing-stone in the middle of a field in Kerry used by cattle to scratch themselves and for passing dogs to piss against.

The young and precocious Seamus Heaney wrote of *the climate of a lost world*; 'a covenant with generations who have been silenced'. My refuge was behind the mangle, Heaney's the top of the dresser: 'The top of the dresser in the kitchen of the house where I lived for the first twelve years of my life was like a Time Machine.'

Ebbing time; time ebbs away.

The crabby old woman stumbling on Belton's avenue was not mother Noelie but daughter Varna, who is half her age, her bloom reduced by incessant labouring, the endless chores of running a farm. Slaughtering day is Wednesday; Pa Percy is seldom seen.

Belton's free-range chicken wrapped in silver foil in the fridge, a bottle of Rioja on the sideboard. Seen through double-glaze glass: the frisky Friesians coming into Clinton Binnions's long field, the pasture as if tilted down to receive them; boom of rising wind in the chimney; rowan saplings scraping against the outer wall with winching seafaring effect. Hills receding into the distance, rain on the way, large live spider in the bath, dead bluebottle on the window-ledge. Biddy busying herself at her chores, three hours twice a week to leave the premises pristine. Three hours paid for are three hours earned; the dignity of labour means 'no cutting corners'. Now I am being charged for lifts into town, so much per mile. Her old banger needs constant servicing.

Biddy begins in the bathroom and when she comes out half an hour later the place is sparkling. Livingroom, kitchen, Dervorgilla's bedroom are Hoovered and swept, every object lifted and every area dusted and polished. My room comes last – the smoking area. I step into the transformed livingroom, the long window wide open on Binnions's field of grazing Friesians being chivvied by Ned's white setter running them and barking, the hills gone further away, the rain nearer.

A glimpse of 'The Ascendancy at Home'.

'A glass of Jameson for the gentleman who just came in!'

Great-hearted Mertull won the Tralee Steeplechase on a track so sodden that the exhausted winner collapsed and died after the race.

When Dervorgilla was in residence the last act of the day, generally a busy one, was to carry the telephone into the bedroom for a good long gossip with a female friend in Ballinaclash; whereas my first act of the day was to kneel in the bathroom and attempt a silent piss into the toilet and then have a stool in the toolshed which had a convenience and handbasin among Dervorgilla's riding and ski equipment, tennis racquets and golf clubs, a sack of Spratt's. Fox covering its tracks.

73

The Eye and Ear Hospital

B y the morning train along the coastline to Dublin and walk to the Eye and Ear Hospital in Adelaide Road, afflicted with not one but two suppurating cysts on the right eyelid and as a natural consequence partially sighted on the right side and feeling queasy and lopsided as though I'd been well and truly hammered in the ring by a merciless opponent.

After the obligatory wait of one hour and a half in the waiting room amid the halt and lame, moving from bench to bench as if awaiting confession in the company of others with eye trouble, I was at last admitted to the inner sanctum where a matronly rolypoly head nurse took charge of me.

I was seated and assured her that my cysts were thoroughly ripe and ready for the knife. Presently in came a brisk young surgeon, a redheaded man hardly thirty, to wash his hands at the basin, humming under his breath.

'Close your little eye now dear,' murmured the matronly nurse and I felt the needle prick, the puncture and the anaesthetic fizz. Take a deep breath and marvel at what you see.

The pasture gleams and blooms, scadoo, scudoo, 'neath bilious clouds that scatter and amass . . . The young surgeon's breathing fanned my face as he probed and probed.

Think on. Deep in a sunlit grove a dragonfly hangs, scudoo, scudoo, like a blue thread loos'd from the sky,

scudoo. Without saying a word to me the young surgeon dug
out two ripe cysts from swooning eyelid. 'That will do nicely,
nurse.' The matronly one washed and bandaged the inflamed
eyelid, winding the bandages about my head like a turban.

I left the hospital feeling weak as a house-fly in midwinter
and made my way to a low-beamed old pub in the purlieus of
Leeson Street bridge for a steadying half-pint of Guinness and
a shot of Jameson.

Then I made it to Merrion Square and the Arts Council
office, where I was not expected, for the scheduled function,
to which I had been invited, was taking place in the Arts Club
in Upper Fitzwilliam Street, whose noble premises I had
already passed, twice, moving in a daze (ever tried walking
about Dublin with wan blind eye?). I felt queasy but walked
on and saw lads playing cricket against a cemetery wall near
Tara Street station, from where I had so oft arrived and
departed when living in Greystones.

I would take the Dart to Bray and wait for a connection to
Wicklow. I would retire to Ballyhara and take it easy.

Two brudders, wan wiff a bad eye.

I stood on the platform at Tara Street and looked with one
eye at the hoardings. Tara Street station was still Tara Street
but the other terminals were renamed after martyrs who had
shed their blood for Ireland. Amiens Street station had
become Connolly station after James Connolly; Kingsbridge
station had become Heuston station after Sean Heuston;
Westland Row (through which I was now passing) becoming
Pearse station after Patrick Pearse the patriot; all executed in
Dublin Castle in the cause of martyrdom and bloodstained
shrouds. And presently there was the sea again on the left and
Sandymount Strand and the house of Heaney out of sight
beyond where philosopher Ussher many times stood
abstracted on the tracks at the level-crossing.

74

The Year Ending

Though the weather forecasts warn of night frosts and first snows have fallen, the mid–November days remain mild. The birds have plenty of food and no need to repair to the feeding tables.

A drenched hawk fiercely tears out the gizzard of a field-mouse on the dripping fence. The valley lies vague in misty haze, Cooney's wood ashiver after a fall of rain.

Yesterday I heard a single gunshot there and asked my authority on things of nature, Ned Ward. Yes, it was he, was him with the high-power rifle putting down a useless dog. 'Poor things,' my brother says, reserving all his pity for dumb creatures. Trying to sleep the other night he heard the crunching of little bones; one of the Russian cats eating a rat or jackdaw.

He is taking his wife to *Pale Rider* tonight.

'Would you not like to come with us?'

But my days of movie-going are over; American movies alarm me, I find the stereophonic sound excessive. After ten minutes I walked out of *To Live and Die in LA*.

The apple tree bare but for a few leaves. A few apples remain rotting on the boughs. Conversation overheard behind partition in the Ancient Mariner:

'I hear she's blind.'

'Ah *course* she's blind. Whaddya tink?'

278

'Dey cudd'na killim!'

Quintessentially gloomy are the Black Castle ruins subsiding into the sea. A billy-goat on its long tether nibbles the tussocks near the broken wall. This is one end of town; funerals leave at a slow pace out the other end.

I heard a ship's siren one morning; then a pheasant's alarm call; post being forced through the letterbox and falling with a soft thud on the carpet where Stella Veronica left muddy footprints. Snow on back ranges of the Wicklow hills lit by the dead sun. Nescafé laced with Jameson to make the hackles rise. Rory's middle period: 'From Numina to Nowhere'. The pheasant goes blundering off through the close-packed young pine wood. A distant dog begins barking.

My brother heard RTE news of a drunken farmer who fell on his back in the midst of his pigs who devoured all but the boots with the feet in them. The pigs were slaughtered and buried with the boots and feet. A perfectly preserved clump of pine roots 3,500 years old and hard as iron has been dug up in Glasnevin, County Offaly.

My brother is reading Thomas De Quincey the opium addict whose brother put to sea. Thomas sailed to Ireland, saw the poverty, the brawling, and the rich going by in carriages. Stella Veronica's legs are getting stiff. 'Do I suffer from arthritis?' The pair of them cycled into Soviet Russia to see Leningrad, the great River Niva, the Hermitage, assailed by mosquitoes big as locusts.

My middle son James is today the same age (twenty-four) as Henry Williamson when *The Sun on the Sands* was published. Williamson rode a Norton motorbike into Devon. Colum reads and rereads Williamson.

The Mayoress of Glenealy wearing her chain of office and medal strides about at the tug-of-war contest. An irate contestant bawls 'Yurra bollicks!' into the face of the flinching referee. Ned Ward and his girl Christina puck a ball about. Darkness falls early; we retire to Kane's pleasant pub in the village.

In the Swiss Alps Dervorgilla swung at the end of a rope. The clouds parted and she looked down. Far below the small and tidy fields of Switzerland were bathed in evening light. 'Lord save us,' breathed Dervorgilla.

26 November

Temperature 40 degrees, snow on hills, difficult to get to sleep, the bed warms slowly with body heat. Heard or imagined a car pulling up on the road outside and smell of cigarettes, rumble of voices planning robbery. The heating comes on at 8 a.m. with a stomach rumble in the pipes. Fresh orange juice and Nescafé laced with Jameson to start the day.

Dervorgilla had spoken of the snowstorm of 1982 and twelve-foot drifts, the icy wind blowing in from the sea and hedges vanishing when she walked the twelve miles to Rathdrum to teach in school.

'You can take down the pictures.'

So I did; and now have bare walls.

Died this year: actress Siobhan McKenna, in Dublin. RIP.

28 November

The Dublin Dunne gang apprehended in Brittas, Garda Superintendent Con Randles on the job. When you get criminal operators with big takes you also get informers. A plainclothes detective gave John Stone a nod and a wink. Notice anything funny about your Sunday clientele? The Dunne gang were sitting there, ordering up expensive drinks; two female Dunnes were caught in the Ladies when McDaniel's closed for the Sunday break. The squad cars arrived soon after. The Dunne gang trades in cocaine. John Stamp wouldn't tell me the Sunday take; but Alex Stone admitted to £5,000.

13 December

Saw sickle moon. Rabbit in fridge, Piat D'Or, presents from Dervorgilla. Gardening gloves from Texas, present from Anastasia, thinking of me cycling in the frost to Brittas.

31 December

House-flies expire on weak legs, mummified daddy-long-legs swings all day on living-room window, swayed by the breeze when I slide open the door that gives on to the valley.

Whenever I feel sad and miss Spain, the scent of pine trees up in the hills above Competa, I put my nose in the hunting-bag of the late Dick Suchman and am back there. Like a whiff of smelling-salts to a neurasthenic. The dry leathery smell of the bag proclaims España.

Would the passes be snowed up?

75

The Road to Arklow

For my last evening in Wicklow I suggested a drink at Lil Doyle's. After supper we drove there and had a good few 'jars' and were among the last to leave at closing time. Stella Veronica took her usual place behind the driver and I sat by her; the empty front passenger seat was for a phantom passenger, who would be riding with us that night.

The brother let in the clutch, or whatever it is you let in (I don't drive) and eased her out into the crossroads, still continuing some engrossing subject covered in the bar, keeping an absent eye fixed on the Arklow Road with little darting glances, but nothing was coming from that direction, or so he judged. But I saw otherwise: a black car shiny as a beetle came hurtling towards us from the Dublin direction; the brother still talking and sniggering, still pulling out, with little quick darting looks in the Arklow direction, in that dreamy state induced by the (for him) unusual pleasant euphoria of gin and lime; or perhaps he was thinking of my imminent departure and how it would be without me. At any rate his mind was elsewhere when the other car hit us broadside on and sent us whirling around until we came to rest by the far ditch, where the engine died.

I felt no brutal jar, no crowbar in the teeth, no fracture of the spine; only the tinkle of broken glass on the tarmac and the Mini groaning in all her meek metalwork. Beside me

Stella Veronica sat still as a statue and the brother uttered no sound. The Mini groaning, glass tinkling on the roadway, the driver rigid and silent, his wife rigid and silent beside me, and I too, as we were whirled around and around – like hobby-horses with nostrils agape and swooning eyeballs, rising up and down to the jiggy oldtime music of the circus merry-go-round carrying the three of us away.

Epilogue and Epigraphs

Memory recalls shattered glass on roadway and on the seat, hubcaps by hedge, bits and pieces of bodywork strewn about on the road, bits that might have been human parts, the Mini being whirled around and the blue ambulance light revolving, and the gardai flashing their torches in but no questions asked, no enquiries as to whether or not we were injured.

We sat there, the three of us huddled together in a strange dreamlike state that was not too alarming nor unpleasant as you might think, the euphoria before extinction, the famous lethargy that attends drowning or freezing to death in the Arctic.

The ambulance driver did not appear nor did the other driver whose black car was far down the Arklow road, and the dumpy woman (not Lil Doyle) who was a dead ringer for our mother (deceased) stood in the lighted doorway of the pub alongside her tall son who had been serving us drinks, staring across at us but making no move, just staring at the wreckage scattered on the road and the car pointing in the wrong direction.

Then Colum was politely asked to step out and walked to and fro in a bemused way, his arm held by the Garda Sergeant who was murmuring into his ear and my brother was nodding.

Back in Ballymona Lodge I took a final steamy bath with
Radox and in bed began to feel the stiffness of my neck, the
difficulty of turning my head; slept well however on my last
night and awoke to find myself surrounded by baggage
packed, overflow of books in large cartons. In Ann Lait's
office I was presented with a staggering final bill.

'Poor Rory is lying on the floor smoking a cigar,' she
laughed down the line.

Poor indeed was Rory now. To Heuston station; stowed
luggage on Cork train waiting on Platform 2. Took a window
seat facing the wrong way, the way I was going; waited to be
whirled off into another life.

The glass doth shew the face whyle thereon one doth look,
But gon, it doth another in lyke manner shew.
Once beeing turn'd away forgotten is the view.

Otto Van Veen 1608

It is singular, how soon we lose the impression of what
ceases to be constantly before us. A year impairs,
a lustre obliterates.

Byron, Journal